T5-CRL-125

Georgia

A Blueprint for Reforms

The World Bank
Washington, D.C.

Copyright © 1993
The International Bank for Reconstruction
and Development/THE WORLD BANK
1818 H Street, N.W.
Washington, D.C. 20433, U.S.A.

All rights reserved
Manufactured in the United States of America
First printing October 1993

World Bank Country Studies are among the many reports originally prepared for internal use
as part of the continuing analysis by the Bank of the economic and related conditions of its
developing member countries and of its dialogues with the governments. Some of the reports are
published in this series with the least possible delay for the use of governments and the
academic, business and financial, and development communities. The typescript of this paper
therefore has not been prepared in accordance with the procedures appropriate to formal printed
texts, and the World Bank accepts no responsibility for errors.

The World Bank does not guarantee the accuracy of the data included in this publication and
accepts no responsibility whatsoever for any consequence of their use. Any maps that accompany
the text have been prepared solely for the convenience of readers; the designations and
presentation of material in them do not imply the expression of any opinion whatsoever on the
part of the World Bank, its affiliates, or its Board or member countries concerning the legal status
of any country, territory, city, or area or of the authorities thereof or concerning the delimitation
of its boundaries or its national affiliation.

The material in this publication is copyrighted. Requests for permission to reproduce portions
of it should be sent to the Office of the Publisher at the address shown in the copyright notice
above. The World Bank encourages dissemination of its work and will normally give permission
promptly and, when the reproduction is for noncommercial purposes, without asking a fee.
Permission to copy portions for classroom use is granted through the Copyright Clearance
Center, 27 Congress Street, Salem, Massachusetts 01970, U.S.A.

The complete backlist of publications from the World Bank is shown in the annual *Index of
Publications,* which contains an alphabetical title list (with full ordering information) and indexes
of subjects, authors, and countries and regions. The latest edition is available free of charge from
the Distribution Unit, Office of the Publisher, The World Bank, 1818 H Street, N.W., Washington,
D.C. 20433, U.S.A., or from Publications, The World Bank, 66, avenue d'Iéna, 75116 Paris, France.

ISSN: 0253-2123

CURRENCY EQUIVALENTS

Currency Unit - Ruble (Rbl)

EXCHANGE RATE: RUBLES PER $

750 (February, 1993)

WEIGHTS AND MEASURES

Metric System

ABBREVIATIONS

CBR	- Central Bank of Russia
CIS	- Commonwealth of Independent States
CMEA	- Council for Mutual Economic Assistance
EPU	- European Payments Union
FSU	- Former Soviet Union
GDP	- Gross Domestic Product
GOSKOMSTAT	- State Committee on Statistics
IMF	- International Monetary Fund
NBG	- National Bank of Georgia
NIP	- National Income Produced
NMP	- Net Material Product
PPP	- Purchasing Power Parity
SPM	- State Property Management Committee
VAT	- Value Added Tax

FISCAL YEAR

January 1 - December 31

Note

This report is based on the work of a mission which visited Tbilisi, Georgia, between June 26 - July 10, 1992. The draft report was discussed with the Georgian authorities in March 1993. The contributors include Messrs/Mdmes. Chandrashekar Pant (mission leader), Marc Chazelas (financial sector), Patrick Conway (macro), Annie Cordet-Dupouy (industry/privatization), Branko Milanovic (social safety net), Arvind Panagariya (trade), Roy Pepper (energy) and Mary Shirley (privatization). Mr. Jamal Saghir contributed to the discussion on privatization and Mr. Kangbin Zheng assisted in the chapter on medium-term prospects. Ms. Alpona Banerji updated the report and the Statistical Appendix. Ms. Frances Rosenthal was responsible for production of the report.

COUNTRY DATA - GEORGIA

GNP per capita in USD in 1991	1640

General
Area (square km)	70,000
Population, 1990 mid-year (thousands)	5,462
Growth rate, 1990 (percent)	0.1
Density, 1990 (per square km)	78

Social Indicators

Population characteristics
Crude birth rate, 1990 (per 1,000)	16.3
Crude death rate, 1990 (per 1,000)	8.7

Health
Infant mortality rate, 1990 (per 1,000 live)	18.9
Life expectancy at birth, 1991	72.6

Net Material Product

	Current Prices (million rubles)		Real Growth Rates (annual % change)	
	1991	1992	1991	1992
NMP at market prices	14,737	82,755	-21	-46
Total consumption	12,866	69,587	-20	-44
Private consumption	11,028	61,472	-23	-42
Government consumption	1,838	8,109	-2	-54
Gross domestic investment	1623	-879	-63	-761
Fixed investment	-92	-1355	-272	..
Change in stocks	1715	476	-108	-579
Net Exports	-89	-6232	..	..
Losses on Fixed Capital	336	20,280	..	..

Output, Employment and Productivity

	NMP in 1991		Employment in 1991		NMP per worker	
	mln rbl	% of total	thousands	% of total	thousand rubles	% of average
Agriculture	4920	33.3	671	39.1	7.3	85
Industry	6148	41.7	488	28.5	12.6	147
Construction	1318	8.9	225	13.1	5.9	69
Transportation & Commun.	553	3.8	104	6.1	5.3	62
Trade & Other Services	1799	12.2	227	13.2	7.9	92
Total	14,737	100.0	1,715	100.0	8.6	100

Government Finance

	Consolidated General Government, 1992	
	mln rbl	% of GDP
Total revenues	18,872	14.0
Total expenditures (including off-budget) 1/	64,947	48.3
Primary budget deficit 2/	47,120	35.1

1/ Excluding interest payments on foreign debt
2/ Including errors and omissions.

Money, Credit and Prices (End of Period) (million rubles)

	1991	1992
Bank Deposit	19,352	78,000
Domestic Credit	31,948	202,000
	Annual Percentage Changes (%)	
Retail Sales Deflator	78.5	913.1

Exports and Imports (million rubles)

	1991	1992
Exports		
Rubble Area	5,287	14,660
Other	51	1,628
Total	5,338	16,289
Imports		
Ruble Area	4,542	18,513
Other	832	3,391
Total	5,374	21,904

CONTENTS

MAP

Text Tables

Text Boxes

Text Figures

EXECUTIVE SUMMARY

Georgia was among the first of the republics of the former Soviet Union (FSU) to declare independence on April 9, 1991. It is a relatively small country with a population of 5.4 million situated in the southern part of the Caucasus region. Until recently, living standards in the republic were quite good. Life expectancy at birth is among the highest in the republics of the FSU, and infant mortality is below the Soviet average, as is the crude death rate. Georgia is known for its large and growing underground economy. This, combined with a strong agricultural economy and a long tradition of close family ties contributes to a picture of a relatively well-off republic. Yet according to official statistics, Georgia ranks near the bottom of the FSU in terms of per-capita income -- with an estimated US$850 in 1992 Georgia ranked higher than only Armenia, Kyrgyzstan and Tadjikistan among the fifteen FSU republics.

Recent Economic Developments

Living standards are being rapidly undermined by the economic crisis that Georgia has been experiencing for the last 18 months. To a large extent this reflects economic developments in other parts of the FSU. The contraction in economic activity and the acceleration in inflation was more a reflection of the progressive break-down of the existing economic system rather than the result of systemic reforms. The restructuring of the economy along lines of comparative advantage is yet to occur.

Net material product (NMP) declined by a cumulative total of 33 percentage points during 1990-91, and fell by an additional 46 percent during 1992. Prices that were more or less stable until 1990 have risen steeply since, increasing by more than 1400 percent on an end-year basis in 1992. Living standards are being further eroded because the shortfall in budgetary revenues has forced the government to cut public expenditures on social programs. More than 116,000 persons (5.4 percent of labor force) are unemployed.

Georgia is particularly vulnerable to developments in Russia since their economies are closely inter-related. More than 67 percent of Georgia's exports went to Russia in 1991, and 60 percent of its imports came from Russia. Georgia depends heavily on imports from Russia for its energy needs: until this year, virtually all crude oil and natural gas consumption was imported from Russia. Not surprisingly, as the Russian economy contracted, so did Georgia's. The disruption of inter-regional trade in 1991-92, and the continuing political turmoil and civil strife in some parts of the country aggravated these negative trends.

Inflation in Georgia also followed trends elsewhere in the region. In 1991 it reflected the excess demand fueled by the monetary overhang that characterized the Soviet economy prior to its dissolution. Thereafter, the increase in prices reflected both a one-shot increase due to the liberalization of most prices in February 1992, and the continuing pressure on demand due to the widening budget deficit and rapid credit expansion, especially in the second half of 1992. The lack of confidence in the ruble added to demand pressures as enterprises and households preferred to spend their money on goods rather than hold it.

Medium Term Prospects

In the next two years, Georgia can only moderate the decline in economic activity. Thereafter, with the right policies and with adequate financial and technical support from the international financial community, the prospects for growth are favorable.

In the near term, the prospects for the Georgian economy are tied closely to Russia's: the linkages in production and demand are simply too strong to be severed quickly without serious damage to the Georgian economy. Since economic activity in Russia is expected to contract further at least until 1994, for this reason alone it is difficult to immediately reverse the decline in economic activity in Georgia. Moreover, as noted earlier, economic restructuring has yet to begin. Experience elsewhere has shown that initially restructuring inevitably results in a contraction in total output: the downsizing of the predominant state sector is not immediately compensated by the growth of the private sector. Thus it is only in 1995 that positive growth may be achieved.

Thereafter, the outlook for the economy is favorable if systemic market oriented reforms are implemented. Georgia has a tradition of entrepreneurship which should serve it well as the economy is unshackled from government controls. It has a potentially strong agriculture where privatization has already had a significant impact on productivity. The service sector can also be expected to respond strongly to the liberalization of the economy. A leaner industrial sector, restructured along lines of comparative advantage and increasingly under private ownership will also contribute to growth in the medium term. With the right policies and adequate financial and technical assistance from the international financial community, Georgia can register growth in the order of 5-6 percent per year during 1995-2003.

The Macroeconomic Policy Framework

Macroeconomic stability is essential for sustained economic recovery. Without it, investor confidence will be lacking. And unless the steady decline in the rate of investment of recent years is reversed, prospects of growth will be limited. Financing the higher rate of investment will require policies to increase the rate of public and private savings. Implementation of a stabilization program, including tight fiscal and credit policies, and complemented by an incomes policy to restrain the growth of wages in the state sector will be essential. These policies, together with adequate external financing will provide the resources necessary for efficient investment.

However, stabilization cannot be sustained unless domestic demand management policies are complemented by systemic reforms that increase the efficiency of resource allocation and minimize the contractionary effects on output of demand management policies. Policies that facilitate and promote inter-regional and international trade are particularly important. Reforms that increase competitiveness and productivity are also necessary if Georgia is to promote its exports, which must provide the main impetus to growth for a small economy such as Georgia.

(I) Stabilization Policies

In view of the continuing instability of the ruble, and the shortages of ruble bank notes that made timely payment of wages and salaries difficult, the government has taken the decision to introduce its own currency (called the Lari). As an interim measure, till adequate preparations are completed to introduce the new currency, coupons were introduced on April 5, 1993.

With the imminent introduction of a new currency, inflation in Georgia will no longer be hostage to imprudent macroeconomic policies in Russia or elsewhere in the ruble zone. However, a new currency per se will not be sufficient to combat inflation. What is important is that adequate policy instruments, and institutions to implement prudent macroeconomic policies, be in place when the new currency is put in circulation.

In order to reduce inflation, a substantial reduction in the budget deficit will be required. In 1992, the primary budget deficit increased to almost 35 percent of GDP, and economic restructuring will only increase the pressure on the budget to finance new needs (for example, additional unemployment, re-capitalization of banks). As experience in other countries has shown, a significant reduction in fiscal imbalances is a necessary element in any successful stabilization episode. The government should aim at balancing the budget in the medium term, starting with a significant initial reduction in the deficit in 1993. This will require policies to increase revenues, but it will also entail cutting all but the most essential public expenditures.

A number of recommendations have been made to mobilize tax revenues. Essentially, these aim at widening the tax base, limiting exemptions and tax holidays, increasing certain tax rates and introducing some new taxes and excises. In addition, measures will be required to strengthen the tax collection and customs administration, especially to cover private business activity and trade that are likely to be the main source of growth in the near future. The progressive liberalization of the economy will also encourage the hitherto under-ground economy to surface, thus increasing the tax base. With respect to expenditures, these were cut sharply in the first half of 1992. However, there is scope for further reductions. Consumer subsidies on food, energy and passenger transport, and rents should be progressively eliminated. Expenditures on various social programs such as pensions, family allowances, unemployment compensation, poverty alleviation can be reduced through better targeting and by reducing the level of some of the benefits. Public investments in the productive branches have also been cut back, although there may be scope for further rationalization.

Even with the best expenditure reduction efforts, the fiscal deficit will remain for the next few years. Increased efforts should be made to finance the deficit by borrowing from the public, say by offering bonds carrying remunerative interest rates. Financing the deficit by credit creation would only increase the pressure on prices and slow down economic recovery.

An incomes policy to restrain the growth of wages in the transition period may also be necessary. In the absence of clear ownership rights and "real" owners, there is no countervailing influence to discipline the wage demands of workers in state enterprises. The growth in wages could outstrip the growth in labor productivity, once again weakening competitiveness. An explicit incomes policy which discourages the excessive growth of wages may be required in the transition until financial discipline is established through privatization and commercialization of state enterprises.

(II) Systemic Reforms

Important systemic reforms to increase productivity and to lay the foundations of a market based economy must be implemented as part of a comprehensive package. Implementing some and not others will not be effective. The government's "Medium Term Program of Macroeconomic Stabilization and Systemic Change in the Republic of Georgia" presents some of the important reforms the government intends to implement in the next 18 months. These reforms include first, measures to progressively liberalize markets for goods and factors of production and thereby reduce government interventions in resource allocation. Continued government intervention in setting prices or limiting profit margins, controlling imports, and directing credits will only perpetuate mis-allocation of resources. Second, systemic reforms are required to encourage and enable enterprises, banks and households to respond flexibly and efficiently to market signals and opportunities. Changes in the ownership and management structure in enterprises and banks is a key aspect of these reforms. In their absence, there is no assurance that agents will not react perversely to market signals. And finally, reforms are necessary to provide an affordable social safety net for those that are poor and for those hurt by the transition. For if this is not in place, the sustainability of reforms could be jeopardized. These three broad areas constitute the agenda for reform. The report addresses the main policy issues in each of these areas and identifies concrete measures that could be implemented in the short and medium term.

As will be seen, the task is enormous. Yet, as in the other countries of the FSU, the capacity to design and implement reforms is limited. Even with the best of technical assistance and training, the pace and breadth of reforms will be constrained by the absorptive capacity of implementing agencies. Thus it is important to define priorities clearly, and to design reforms so that they are relatively easy to implement. At this stage, simplicity in design should take precedence over complicated and sophisticated approaches. For this reason as well, reforms that call for the withdrawal of the state from economic activity must have priority.

A second criteria for choosing priorities, and sequencing, must be whether or not (and how seriously) the proposed reform strengthens or weakens the fiscal balance. As argued earlier, achieving macroeconomic stability is critical and the reduction of fiscal imbalances is a key to achieving this objective. Reforms that increase tax revenues, or reduce claims on government resources, should have priority, at least in the short term.

A third criteria should be whether or not the reforms seek to harness the latent entrepreneurial talent of the Georgian people. There is some evidence suggesting the likelihood of considerable, and thriving, unreported economic activity. Bringing this sector into the mainstream of economic activity, and fostering its growth, is likely to have a strong ripple effect throughout the economy. Policies that promote this end, including in particular measures that reduce government intervention in economic activity, should be accorded priority.

Policies to Intensify Competition

The government has already taken the first major step towards liberalizing the economy by freeing most retail prices. It should move quickly to eliminate price controls on some of the other commodities. Forces of competition should be strengthened by eliminating barriers to trade, domestic and foreign, and by facilitating entry of new enterprises. Measures to facilitate inter-regional trade, such as a clearing union, could be useful during the transition period.

Prices of only a few basic foods, public utilities and rent are controlled by the government. Rightly, the government has also moved to remove barriers to trade in commodity markets, including limits on profit margins in trade. However, competition is still limited and additional measures will be required. These include eliminating barriers to competition from imports, and deregulation policies to encourage entry of new enterprises. A state-supervised policy of soliciting competitive bids for the distribution of commodities to the market may also be desirable to promote competition in the transition.

Prices that remain administered have been raised several-fold since January 1992. However, at the current exchange rate, they still remain below world prices. Of special importance are energy prices. Some energy prices have been liberalized (gasoline, diesel oil, and crude oil). However, others remain administered. The bulk of energy consumed in Georgia is imported, and even with the recent increases in domestic energy prices, they sell at substantially below the import costs. Notwithstanding adjustments in the exchange rate, further increases in energy prices are likely to be required not only to economize on the use of energy (energy intensity is relatively high in Georgia), but also to ease the pressure on the budget. With some import prices still below world prices, further increases in domestic energy prices cannot be avoided.

For a small economy like Georgia, international trade provides a potent stimulus for competition. While the import regime is already quite free, exports are restricted through a pervasive licensing system. This should be substantially eliminated.

An even bigger problem in the short to medium term is to prevent a further collapse of inter-regional trade. The continuing uncertainty about the currency regime in Georgia and elsewhere in the region, together with the uncertainty about the value of the ruble, is forcing countries to shift increasingly to barter trade, or to balance trade bilaterally. This will only further shrink the volume of trade, with adverse impact on production and welfare throughout the region. In these circumstances, a clearing union providing short-term credit and having relatively short settlement periods may help preserve inter-regional trade.

Enterprise Reform

Reforms that expose the economy to competition and market forces are important but are not sufficient to improve the efficiency in resource allocation. Liberalization does not, by itself, provide the structures that are part and parcel of the checks and balances inherent to a well-functioning market economy (e.g., atomistic markets, property rights, binding contracts, public regulations etc). Without these structures, incentives may operate in perverse ways -- to the detriment of efficiency. Creating the legal and institutional structures that go with a market economy must be on top of the government's priorities.

One of the most fundamental issue to be resolved is the question of property rights. While it is probably possible to run a clear cut state enterprise or a private firm efficiently, it is not possible to get anything like efficiency from an enterprise whose current and future ownership status are in limbo. Thus it is important, first, to identify as quickly as possible those activities and enterprises that are to be privatized, and those that will remain under state ownership even in the long term. Second, it is important to identify the "real" owner right away, and eliminate any ambiguity about who the owner is. Without clearly defined ownership rights, and legally recognized owners with an interest in the long term preservation and appreciation of the enterprises' capital, there is no discipline on enterprise managers, and little incentive for them to improve productivity. Privatization of state enterprises, whereby ownership of assets is transferred to clearly identified owners, is therefore of critical importance.

How to accelerate privatization while maintaining transparency of the process becomes an immediate policy issue.

In contrast to many other countries of the FSU, Georgia has already successfully privatized most of public housing. It has also privatized more than 50 percent of agricultural land. In mid-August 1992, the government adopted the first State Program of Privatization of State and Municipality Owned Enterprises for 1992-93. It defines the government's strategy for privatization, the scope of privatization, and institutional arrangements to implement the program. Except for water and forestry resources and certain public utilities (such as large power plants, pipelines, and the metro), virtually everything else is to be privatized over time. The government also approved the first list of 752 enterprises and assets that are to be sold by mid-1993. These include enterprises of different sizes. However little progress has been achieved to date in the privatization of small or large enterprises. The first small scale auction was held in Tbilisi in early March but this involved only the sale of cars and trucks. Auctions of small shops, catering services and unfinished construction projects in Tbilisi began in the first half of 1993.

Rightly, the government intends to adopt a flexible and pragmatic strategy, combining a top-down and a bottom-up approach. Simple, pragmatic and flexible approaches should be preferred to sophisticated first best solutions. Speed is important. The decentralized, bottom-up approach, where privatization is initiated by the workers, managers, or a potential buyer, is especially appropriate given the limited implementation capacity of the official agencies. However, it is important that there be transparent rules and regulations governing the process. Otherwise, as experience elsewhere has shown, there is a danger that accelerated privatization schemes result in abuse and asset stripping (as happened in Poland and Hungary in the early stages of spontaneous privatization).

The government is considering a voucher scheme to accelerate the privatization of medium and large state enterprises and to ensure widespread ownership. The goal is to distribute the first tranche of vouchers in 1993. Initially, enterprises with an estimated book value greater than Rbl 20 million will be transformed into joint stock companies and partially privatized through the distribution of vouchers.

Preparatory work and important policy decisions with regard to the implementation of the voucher scheme are yet to be finalized. Any scheme should take account of the following considerations. First, the scheme should be simple. Complex share distribution schemes should be avoided in favor of distributing the vouchers free to the population. Second, the objective of achieving widespread ownership should be balanced with the need to provide effective ownership control. Only a limited portion (say 30 percent) of the total assets should be distributed through the voucher scheme. For the same reason, not more than, say, 20 percent of assets should be distributed to employees. Further, the voucher scheme should be designed to allow sales to controlling shareholders. In particular, it would be desirable that vouchers be tradable, thus permitting consolidation of ownership. In order to reduce the inflationary impact of tradable vouchers, these may be issued in tranches that are tradable for a limited duration only.

As experience in Poland, Hungary and Czechoslovakia has shown, even the best of privatization takes time, and there are certain activities that are unlikely to be privatized even in the long term (for example, public utilities). For these activities, alternative governance structures must be created that work within the existing state ownership but make management and workers sensitive to long-term profitability considerations. One solution which is being increasingly adopted in other countries is commercialization of enterprises. The government's strategy recognizes the importance of corporatization, but the process of corporatization is not well defined nor is it indicated which companies will be transformed and the criteria for transformation. In order to accelerate corporatization, it is desirable that the government adopt a decree on the immediate transformation into joint stock companies of all enterprises employing, for example, more than 150-200 people. The state would exercise its ownership rights in the transformed joint stock companies through company boards. For this to work, however, there ought to be significant incentive for managers and directors to manage the enterprise well.

Financial discipline will have to be tightened if enterprise managers and workers are to be sensitive to market signals. Subsidies to loss-making activities, financed through the budget or through the financial system, will have to be progressively reduced. To the extent subsidies are provided during a transition period, these should be done through the budget, which is transparent, rather than through the financial system. These subsidies should be eliminated over time, as part of an overall restructuring plan for these enterprises. The closure of a few obviously loss-making activities may be necessary.

While the state enterprises will continue to dominate the productive branches in the short to medium term, the main source of growth during this period will be the small but dynamic private sector. The enactment of new legislation on the creation and transfer of property rights and on contract law, as well as their enforcement, is essential to the development of the private sector. Other measures may also be required. Macroeconomic stabilization, the liberalization of prices and trade, the reform of the financial sector, and the elimination of support to the state enterprise sector will also facilitate the growth of the private sector.

Financial Sector Reforms

An efficient financial system is necessary to mobilize financial saving of the population and channel it to efficient investors. Currently, the banking system is not performing either of these functions adequately. Financial institutions offer little incentive to saving. And a large part of financial savings of the population is being directed to particular activities by the state without regard to the profitability of the investments.

Savings deposits in banks are shrinking in nominal and real terms. This is not surprising: interest rates on savings deposits are too low. There is little incentive for banks to raise these rates as long as they have access to low cost refinancing credits from the NBG. Thus, interest rates on refinancing credits from the NBG should be raised to at least the maximum deposit interest rate. Interest rates on household deposits with the savings bank should also be increased. But raising interest rates may not be sufficient to promote savings in banks. To increase public confidence in the banking system it may be necessary to eliminate the limits on withdrawal of savings deposits.

Most of the credit expansion in 1992 by the major banks was based on refinance credits from the NBG. These were used to finance priority projects chosen by the NBG based on recommendations of the government. Directed credits are not consistent with a decentralized, market based financial system. Their use should be phased out, and banks should be encouraged to obtain resources from the inter-bank market. Access to refinance credits should be based on clear criteria (such as the capital of the bank). It should not distinguish between different activities.

Banks are burdened by a large portfolio of non-performing loans. This is partly due to the loss of certain assets resulting from the break-up of the FSU. Partly it is caused by the policy of the government which directed the banks to lend to clients that were not creditworthy. The burden of non-performing loans is only likely to worsen as interest rates rise and enterprise restructuring gets underway. Non-performing loans skew the lending decisions of banks towards high risk investments. Unless prudential regulations are strong, there is a risk of financial instability. This risk is even greater given the incestuous relationship between banks and enterprises. Banks are largely owned by enterprises that are also its major clients, which makes objective portfolio decision-making difficult.

Prudential regulations, and the capacity to supervise banks effectively, need to be strengthened urgently. To reduce risks, it would be desirable to lower the maximum amount of credit any one client can get from 50 percent of the paid in capital to 15-20 percent. Currently, prudential regulations do not apply to state banks which dominate the financial system. An action plan to force state banks to comply with prudential regulations should be adopted. The licensing requirements for new banks should be tightened by increasing the minimum capital requirement, by lowering the maximum individual shareholding limit, and by raising financial and managerial standards for founders. In the short term, problem banks should be downsized. Over the medium term, the problem of non-performing loans would need to be addressed through recapitalization, in the context of the restructuring and privatization of banks.

Reform of the Social Safety Net

The restructuring of the economy will cause hardship for the population during the transition. Unemployment will rise significantly, real wages are bound to fall, and the cuts in consumer subsidies will increase the cost of living. Unless these adverse consequences are managed carefully, social support for the reform process will be jeopardized. However, resources are scarce. Tax rates are already quite high and increasing these further can only hurt Georgian competitiveness at a time when export competitiveness is essential. Increasing taxes will also prevent the underground economy from surfacing, which should be an important objective of reforms. Moreover, increasing the rates may not mean much anyway if tax collection does not improve. On the other hand, the scope for deficit financing is also limited given the necessity of stabilizing inflation. Thus there is no option but to economize on social spending by targeting these to the most needy, and by reducing the level of some of the existing benefits. The report recommends concrete ways in which savings can be achieved in each of the main social programs: pensions and family allowances, sick pay, and unemployment compensation. Roughly, total spending on these programs was equivalent to 12-13 percent of GDP.

Expenditures on pensions can be reduced by reducing payments to working pensioners and by tightening the eligibility criteria for obtaining disability pensions. These two categories of pensioners are very large in Georgia compared to other countries. A gradual increase in the retirement age of men (from 60 to 62 years) and for women (from 55 to 62 years) may also be desirable. Sick leave benefits are also generous: 100 percent of the wage for up to 5 months of leave for all those with 8 years seniority. The level of the benefit should be reduced to say 80 percent of the wage and the number of days reduced (the average number of days of sick leave in most economies is 15-20 per year). Also, to reduce the scope for abuse, enterprises should bear the cost of at least the first week of sick leave.

By end 1992, about 116,000 persons (5.4 percent of labor force) were unemployed, though only 10.5 percent of the unemployed workers received unemployment benefits. Entitlements are relatively generous: they imply an average replacement rate (benefits as a share of previous wage) of 65 percent which is in the upper ranges of the ratio in eastern and western Europe. If restructuring occurs at about the pace at which it did in some of the East European economies during 1990-91 (for example Poland, Czechoslovakia), the rate of unemployment (and those eligible for benefits) could rise very quickly to at least 8 percent (12-13 percent in Slovakia). If this happens, the existing payroll tax of 3 percent will be insufficient to finance the existing level of unemployment compensation. Either the payroll tax would have to be increased, or present entitlements reduced substantially. A combination of reduction in present levels of unemployment entitlements (so as to reduce the replacement rate to about 50 percent), plus the savings generated from reforms in pensions, sick pay etc. would permit financing of unemployment benefits without raising the payroll tax. One way to reduce present entitlements would be to lower the benefits during the first three months of unemployment from the present level of 100 percent of the previous wage to, for example, 70 percent. Unemployment benefits for people released from jails, the army, and new job entrants should also be eliminated.

While these proposals are likely to be sufficient to ensure that the increased claims for unemployment compensation can be met without raising taxes, they will not be adequate to provide funds for any kind of universal welfare scheme. The poverty gap is likely to be too large. The best that can be expected in the short term is continued recourse to foreign funding and some ad-hoc help to the most destitute along the lines of what already exists (help for refugees, food aid). In order to deliver such help more effectively, a denser network of local (community-based) institutions should be developed. However, if a more universal welfare system is desired, the only alternative is a substantial increase in the already-high taxation.

External Financing Requirements

Economic recovery will depend on the implementation of the stabilization policies and structural reforms outlined above. However, it will also require external financial and technical assistance. Without such support, as mentioned above, the drop in living standards is likely to be too steep, which could jeopardize social support for the reform program. External financial assistance will also be needed to finance critical imports for production as well as technical assistance in designing and implementing the transition to a market economy.

Conservatively, it is estimated Georgia will require about $250-350 million per year during 1993-95. This assumes Georgia will not have to service any of its share of FSU debt during the period. Almost all of this foreign capital inflow must most likely come from official bilateral and multilateral sources. Over time, as macroeconomic stability is ensured and structural reforms take hold, it may be expected that commercial sources of financing will increase their exposure. Given the uncertainties underlying the medium term, creditworthiness assessments are fraught with pitfalls. What is clear, however, is that Georgia presently faces a serious economic and financial crisis. To weather this successfully, external technical and financial assistance in the short term must contain a substantial grant element.

To facilitate foreign capital inflow, and to use it effectively, the government will need to develop adequate institutional capacity. This will involve establishing a capacity to define priorities for external financial and technical assistance; identifying alternative sources for assistance; coordinating the activities of different donors; managing external debt; and maintaining a close link between economic policy management and external financing needs.

PART I

THE IMPERATIVE OF MACROECONOMIC STABILIZATION

The collapse of the Soviet Union in late 1991 and the attendant disruption in institutions that managed the economy till then has forced the Georgian economy into a tailspin. Output contracted by a cumulative 33 percent during 1990 and 1991 and NMP declined by another 46 percent in 1992. Inflation accelerated to more than 1400 percent by end-1992. It is in these difficult conditions that Georgia is attempting to establish the foundations of a market economy. The task is especially daunting because Georgia starts the transformation virtually from scratch: existing institutions are ill-suited to a market based economy, and there is a dearth of people who know and understand how the transition to a market economy is to be managed. Yet, unlike many of the other countries of the FSU, Georgia has a long tradition of entrepreneurship which should serve it well during the transition (Chapter 1).

As described in Chapter 2, the medium term prospects for the economy are good, based on robust growth in exports. There is a solid potential in agriculture, and services (including tourism) are likely to develop strongly. With appropriate macroeconomic stabilization policies and structural reforms, this potential can be achieved. However, in the short term the decline in output can only be moderated, not reversed. And macroeconomic stabilization policies will be essential to decelerate the rate of inflation. This will require maintaining tight fiscal, credit and incomes policies (Chapter 3).

Georgia will require considerable external financial assistance, with a substantial degree of concessionality, at least initially, if it is to successfully manage the transition. This is needed to help cushion the decline in private consumption and to raise the rate of investment. Already, living standards have fallen steeply making Georgia one of the poorer countries of the FSU. And the future growth of the economy is being jeopardized by the continuing cuts in public and private investment. Concessional external assistance can help reverse these trends and thus sustain the transition during a difficult period.

CHAPTER 1

The Origins of the Crisis

Background

Georgia is a relatively small country with a population of 5.4 million. Covering an area of 70,000 square kilometers, it is situated in the southern part of the Caucasus region, bordered by Turkey and Armenia to the southwest, Azerbaijan to the southeast, and Russia on the north. The Black sea borders Georgia on the west.[1]

Georgia's per capita income is estimated at $850 in 1992, which places it among the poorer republics of the former Soviet Union (FSU).[2] However, other indicators of living standards belie this assessment: life expectancy at birth is the highest among the republics, and infant mortality is below the FSU average, as is the crude death rate. Despite a high population density, Georgia has a stock of housing per capita that is unrivaled outside the Baltic states (see Table 1.1, Statistical Appendix). One explanation for this puzzle may be the existence of a thriving underground economy. Georgia has a long history of non-official market transactions and the existence of a relatively prosperous under-ground economy, not captured by official statistics, is consistent with the observed standard of living.

Agriculture is relatively more important in the Georgian economy than in other economies of the FSU. It accounted for about 29 percent of Net Material Product (NMP) in 1992, while industry contributed another 34 percent.[3] The rest of NMP was divided between transport and communication (21 percent), construction (8 percent), trade and catering (2 percent) and others (Table 2.2, Statistical Appendix). Georgia produced almost the entire citrus fruits and tea crops of the FSU, and a disproportionately large share of grapes. While industry has a substantial agro-industrial base, Georgia was also a relatively large producer of steel pipes, electric motors, synthetic fibers, roofing material, textiles and shoes. There is significant private sector activity in agriculture and already more than 50 percent of agricultural land is privately owned. Industry is almost entirely state-owned.

External trade, largely with the republics of the FSU, plays a big role in the economy. Total external trade (the average of imports and exports) amounted to almost 43 percent of GDP in 1988-90, of which inter-republican trade was as much as 37 percent of GDP (Table 3.1, Statistical Appendix).[4] Georgia relies heavily on imports of energy from other republics, notably Russia (for electricity, crude oil) and Turkmenistan (natural gas). Imported energy amounted to about 80 percent of total energy supply in 1990. Wheat, sugar and some heavy machinery are the other major imports. Georgia's main exports include citrus, tea, tobacco, wine and mineral water. By far the biggest trading partner is Russia. Georgia was a net beneficiary in trade with the rest of the FSU primarily due to the subsidization of energy imports.

Traditionally, Georgia has recorded a trade surplus with the republics and a deficit with the rest of the world. However, because energy imports from Russia were under-priced, trade with the republics would also very likely have been in deficit if it were valued at international prices.[5]

Recent Economic Developments

Recent macroeconomic developments reflect both trends that are common to the other republics of the FSU (especially Russia) as well as the peculiarities of the Georgian experience. All the countries of the FSU experienced a sharp contraction in output during 1990-92 as well as accelerating inflation. So has Georgia. The shrinking of inter-regional trade has affected not only Georgia but every other republic of the FSU. And Georgia suffers from the same shortage of ruble banknotes as do the other countries in the region.

On the other hand, recent developments were influenced by factors specific to Georgia. First, there is probably more of an underground economy in Georgia than in other republics (Box 1.1). The existence of the underground economy, and its apparent growth in recent years, may have helped cushion the impact of the collapse of the official economy. And the traditional entrepreneurial skills provide Georgia a distinct advantage over many of the other countries in the region in their transition to a market economy. Second, Georgia suffered more than other republics because it was the first to break away from the Soviet Union, which led to harsh retaliation in the form of limitations on trade of critical imports. Third, given Georgia's relatively small size, and its greater dependence on trade, the breakdown of trade that occurred in 1991-92 affected Georgia relatively more strongly. Trends in Russia are likely to be magnified in Georgia: just as economic contraction will be more severe than in Russia, economic recovery will be quicker as well. And finally, unlike most of the other republics Georgia suffered from natural disasters and civil disturbances in 1991-92.

Output

After a long period of sustained growth during the seventies and until the mid-eighties, production in Georgia has been steadily declining since 1989. NMP fell in 1990 and 1991 by a cumulative total of almost 33 percent. The decline in economic activity accelerated in 1992, when NMP fell by 46 percent. Industrial production is estimated to have fallen by more than 34 percent in 1992 and agricultural production by about 49 percent. The decline in production was pretty much across the board. (see Tables 2.3 and 7.1, Statistical Appendix).

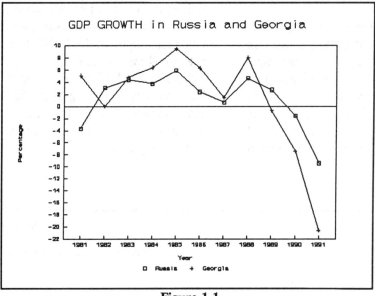

Figure 1.1

This decline was caused by several factors. First, to a large extent the decline in Georgia mirrors the decline in economic activity in Russia (Figure 1.1). After stagnating in 1990, GDP in Russia fell by 9 percent in 1991 and by a further 15 percent during 1992. Georgia depends on Russia for supplies of critical inputs in production (such as energy) as well as a source of demand for its products.[6] Second, there was a precipitous decline of inter-regional trade, caused partly by the general disarray in the Soviet Union during 1990-91, but also by the blockage of Georgia after independence in 1991 and continuing strained relations with Russia. Imports of critical imports, especially oil and natural gas from Russia were cut sharply, affecting majority of industry, agriculture and transport.[7] Third, Georgia experienced a deterioration in its terms of trade as prices of critical inputs (energy, fertilization, ores) that Georgia imported from Russia increased sharply.[8]

The collapse of output was also caused by factors specific to Georgia. First, the earthquake in April 1991 caused extensive damage to infrastructure and had an adverse impact on production (particularly agriculture). Second, severe shortages of energy developed towards the end of 1991 because of the harsh winter (which increased demand and reduced hydroelectric production), disruption of some imports (because of the conflict between Armenia and Azerbaijan), and the difficulties of concluding inter-state agreements on energy imports because of sharply increased prices. Finally, the political tensions and civil strife in parts of Georgia contributed to the loss in production.[9]

Inflation

As in the other parts of the FSU, in Georgia too price stability was maintained until 1990. But with the collapse of the system in 1991, inflation accelerated sharply. The retail sales deflator rose by 78.5 percent during 1991 (up from 4.8 percent during 1990). Indeed, comparing the fourth quarter of 1991 with the same period of 1990, the index rose by 128 percent. Inflation continued to accelerate in 1992, especially during the second half. While the average yearly increase in the retail price index was about 913 percent, prices rose 36 percent in December alone.

The acceleration of inflation can be attributed to the continuing contraction in supply on the one hand and the release of pent up demand pressures on the other. On the supply side, there was not only a sharp contraction in real output in 1991 (NMP fell by 21 percent), but also a significant reduction in net imports (from Rbl 864 million in 1990 to only Rbl 36 million in 1991, in current prices). These combined to reduce domestic availability of goods.[10] On the demand side, excess demand pressures were fueled by the monetary overhang that characterized the Soviet Union prior to its dissolution: as controls weakened somewhat in 1991, prices rose as the population rid itself of its excess money holdings.[11] Demand was also fueled by the marked increase in the fiscal deficits of the national and local governments and its monetary financing.[12]

Retail Prices 1990-92

Percentage Change over comparable period in preceding year

| | 1990 | 1991 | 1992 | | | | | | | | | | | |
	Annual	Annual	J	F	M	A	M	J	J	A	S	O	N	D
General Index	4.8	78.5	178	217	788	827	637	777	911	970	1033	1098	1202	1463

Source: Table 8.1, Statistical Appendix

The government budget deteriorated from a surplus of 1.3 percent of GDP in 1990 (which was possible in part due to net transfers from the Union of about 5 percent of GDP) to a deficit of about 3.5 percent of GDP in 1991.[13] The poor fiscal performance was caused both by shortfalls in revenue (due to greater than expected decline in production and worsening tax collection) and increased expenditures (due to payment for earthquake damage, wage increases, and substantial subsidies for bread and other staples).[14] The deficit was financed partly by currency issued by the Soviet State Bank (currency in circulation increased by Rbl 3.2 billion, or 108 percent in 1991). The remainder was largely financed by accumulating arrears (e.g., to suppliers, wages, social security payments). (Table 4.1, Statistical Appendix).

Figure 1.2

The surge in retail prices in March 1992 reflected the liberalization of most prices in February 1992, and the steep increase in prices that remained under the control of the state thereafter[15] (Table 8.4, Statistical Appendix). These price adjustments had a one-shot impact on the level of prices in 1992, and may have wiped out the monetary overhang.[16] What explains the continuing pressure on prices? First, controlled prices continued to be increased throughout 1992. Prices of energy (electricity, natural gas, LPG) were raised substantially in October 1992. Milk prices increased 60 fold in 1992 and the price of bread was raised 100 fold. Second, on the supply side, as in 1991, domestic availability of goods remained scarce as output fell sharply and net imports declined further. Moreover, the continuing uncertainty and inflationary expectations created incentives to withhold production from the market in anticipation of higher prices.

On the demand side, the widening budget deficit continued to exert pressure on prices. The increase in the budget deficit was due to both shortfalls in revenue (due partly to the disruptive effects of the civil conflict) as well as the rapid growth of expenditures, especially in the second half of the year.[17] Despite efforts to mobilize additional revenues,[18] they fell from about 30 percent of GDP in 1991 to only about 14 percent in 1992. And while serious efforts were made to curtail government expenditures

Subsidies and Transfers		
	Rbl million	
	1992 budget	*Jan-May 1992 Actual*
Energy		
- Natural gas	1013	440
- Coal	200	85
Construction	1727	381
Transportation	266	117
Agriculture	574	n.a.

during the first half of the year (see table above), expenditures increased sharply thereafter reaching about 48 percent of GDP by the fourth quarter. The deficit was financed almost entirely by bank credit (Table 4.1, Statistical Appendix).

Box 1.1
Is there an Expanding Underground Economy?

The evidence suggests that there is a substantial underground economy not reflected in official production statistics, but contributing to a more comfortable lifestyle than indicated by official statistics alone.[a]

A number of factors suggest a growing underground economy. **First**, the amount of credit creation during the eighties exceeded that consistent with reported production. Assuming that the ratio of credit to national income produced (NIP) in Georgia is the same as the average for the Soviet Union, the actual use of credit in Georgia implies that NIP is consistently higher than official estimates. Moreover, the gap is widening: by 1990, the NIP is 63 percent higher than the official estimates (see figure). **Second**, the savings behavior is at odds with the officially reported income. While Georgia ranked 12th poorest among the 15 republics of the FSU in terms of their per capita income in 1991 (with per capita income higher than that in Kyrgyzstan, Tadjikistan, and Uzbekistan), savings deposits per capita in Georgia (Rbl 1773 million) were high compared to most of the republics (with the exception of Russia, Belarus, Lithuania, Armenia and Ukraine). **Third**, a significant proportion of the working population in Georgia is engaged in agriculture, and an increasing share of farmers' income is coming from private sources, which is typically hard to measure. In 1990, almost 45 percent of farmers' income came from private farming and an additional 8 percent from other (mostly private) sources. Compared to the mid-1980s the importance of private sector income for farmers increased by 8 percentage points (Data derived from Budgets of Farmers and Workers, Cabinet of Economic Affairs, Supreme Council of Georgia, Tbilisi, 1991). **Fourth**, Georgia (along with Azerbaijan) recorded the highest incidence of absenteeism (in terms of percent of scheduled workhours) in the republics of the FSU in 1990, pointing to participation in underground activities.

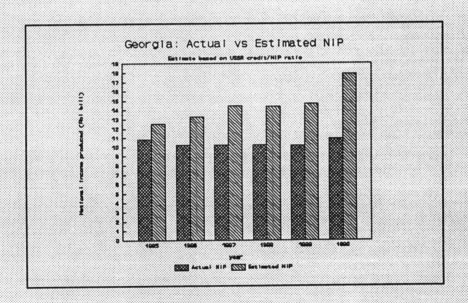

Georgia: Actual vs Estimated NIP
Estimate based on USSR credit/NIP ratio

[a] This is not a new phenomenon for Georgia. As Grossman (1977) put it, "[In underground activities] Georgia has a reputation second to none. ...In form this activity may not differ greatly from what takes place in other regions, but in Georgia it seems to have been carried out on an unparalleled scale and with unrivaled scope and daring. Grossman, G.: "The 'Second Economy' of the USSR", Problems of Communism 26, pp. 25-40. Suny (1988) reports that only 68 percent of agricultural production in 1970 was sold to official markets, as opposed to 97 percent in neighboring Armenia. Suny, R.: The Making of the Georgian Nation. Bloomington, IN: Indiana University Press, 1988.

In the first six months of 1992, the NBG was quite effective in limiting credit creation: despite an inflation rate of over 500 percent, total domestic credit increased by only 66 percent. Thereafter, however, monetary policy was very expansionary. Domestic credit increased by more than 280 percent between June and December 1992, while prices rose by a cumulative 145 percent. Credit expansion was equally rapid to the state government and to public enterprises. (Table 5.1, Statistical Appendix).

Trade

Georgia's economy is closely linked to the FSU: 96 percent of the country's exports went to the FSU, and imports from that region constituted 72 percent of total imports in 1990. Since 1990, trade with the republics of the FSU and with the rest of the world has declined precipitously. In 1991, the value of total imports and exports from the ruble area fell by 8 percent while the value of trade with the rest of the world declined by 59 percent. (Table 3.1, Statistical Appendix). Since prices rose steeply in 1991, the decline in nominal values reflects a much steeper decline in the real volume of trade. These trends were heightened in 1992.

In addition to the decline in the **volume** of trade, Georgia experienced a sharp deterioration in **terms of trade**. This mainly reflected the fact that (i) Georgia is a net energy importer: imports of energy amounted to approximately 80 percent of total available energy resources in 1990; and (ii) import prices for energy have increased sharply in the last two years.[19] Even with these price increases, import prices remain below world prices: a further deterioration in terms of trade is likely in the coming years as import prices get closer to world prices.[20]

Financial Crisis

In common with other countries belonging to the ruble zone, Georgia also suffered from a severe "shortage" of ruble banknotes. The features of this shortage are strikingly similar in different countries: producers and governments have too little access to currency through their bank accounts, and thus cannot pay cash for wages, pensions, and suppliers of intermediate inputs. Wage earners and pensioners have insufficient currency to make necessary purchases, forcing producers to shut down or accumulate arrears with suppliers. Suppliers in turn are forced to shut down, or accumulate arrears with labor or their own suppliers. To alleviate this shortage, the government has sharply limited the access of depositors to their savings accounts. The shortage of rubles has also added impetus to pressures for introducing a separate currency.

The currency shortage may be a manifestation of financial disintermediation: the share of savings in NMP fell from 70.4 percent in end 1990 to 6.9 percent by end May 1992 (for details see Box 1.2). The shortage of currency begins with the financial system and affects those sectors that rely most on the organized financial system. Savers are reluctant to place their currency in savings deposits, with the result that the financial system has few ruble notes when the government, or state sector producers, draw down their account or take out a loan to finance their payroll or purchase of inputs. This leads to the accumulation of arrears, and the observed premium for cash in the banking system.

The currency shortage could be alleviated by implementing policies to reverse the process of financial disintermediation. This was demonstrated strikingly in July 1992, when the government announced that the value of all accounts held in the Saving Bank would be doubled in two weeks. The response was dramatic: there was an inflow of cash equivalent to Rbl 5 billion, nearly equal to the existing stock of deposits. This is strong support to the contention that the quantity of money is not insufficient; rather, the rate of return on savings deposits is. Policies to limit saving withdrawal serve only to further undermine the confidence in the banking system and will make the cash shortage worse.

Despite the recent inflow of cash due to the doubling of the value of saving deposits, the Saving Bank remains illiquid. Rather than build up reserves, the cash that was attracted into the system was transferred to other banks who lent it to their various clients. Consequently, the Savings Bank remains under siege by the depositors, whose savings accounts are still illiquid.

Thus to summarize, the economy is in a crisis. Real GDP declined by 46 percent in 1992. And the average yearly inflation rate accelerated to over 913 percent (1463 percent on an end-year basis). The budget deficit is out of control because revenues have shrunk to a fraction of what they used to be and public spending was not cut correspondingly. Yet some public expenditures have been cut drastically, necessitating scaling down of essential social programs and public investment in critical infrastructure. Were it not for the apparent growth of the underground economy, the situation would have been worse.

To a large extent, these developments were outside the control of the authorities. Given the close inter-connection between the Georgian economy and the economies of the republics of the FSU (especially Russia), the collapse of the Soviet system was bound to hurt the Georgian economy. Indeed, given its relatively small size, trends in the Russian economy are likely to be magnified in Georgia. Other factors, including the autarkic policies of the previous government, the earthquake in 1991 and the continuing civil strife in parts of the country contributed to the economic woes in Georgia. What is clear is that the recent poor performance of the economy cannot be attributed to economic reforms. They are more a reflection of the breakdown of institutions and policies that served the previous command economy.

The government is beginning to respond to the crisis. Rightly, stabilization policies are being accorded priority. The government has also initiated important systemic reforms. Policies to promote free trade, and to encourage entrepreneurship will be especially important for a successful transition.

Box 1.2
The Cash Shortage Phenomenon

A number of the members of the ruble currency zone has reported a continuing shortage of currency in circulation. The features of this "cash shortage" are strikingly similar across countries: producers and government have too little access to currency through their financial accounts, and thus cannot pay wages, pensions and intermediate-input suppliers in cash. Wage-earners and pensioners then receive insufficient currency to make necessary purchases, while producers must shut down or run arrears with suppliers. These suppliers in turn have no currency, and must either shut down or run arrears with their labor and suppliers. The problem is exacerbated by the rapid rise in retail prices throughout the ruble zone. In the financial intermediaries a premium arises, with non-cash rubles (i.e., accounting credits at financial intermediaries) selling at a discount to cash rubles.

Policies to date to deal with this problem have focused on adding currency to circulation or raising the velocity of currency. In Russia, President Yeltsin's most popular announcements are those of an airlift of currency to beleaguered financial districts. In Kazakhstan the National Bank of Kazakhstan (NBK) has instituted strict limits on cash withdrawals from savings accounts to maintain cash balance for other transactions. The Kazakhstan government has also introduced direct payments of wages to savings accounts as well as checking operations for consumers in an attempt to restrict the reliance of transactions on currency. In Georgia, National Bank of Georgia (NBG) directives have very sharply limited the access of depositors to their savings accounts as well. Both Georgia and Kazakhstan have appealed repeatedly and emotionally to the Central Bank of Russia (CBR) for inflows of currency, and in Georgia's case paid a 21 percent premium to receive currency — a concrete example of the premium for cash in the banking system.

The three popular explanations of the cash shortage can be illustrated through the quantity equation $Mv = PY$, with M the money supply, v the velocity of money, P the price index and Y the real value of goods entering transactions. The first states that the price index has simply risen too high with price liberalization — so high in fact that despite the fall in availability of goods, with constant v there is insufficient currency to satisfy the equation.[a] There has been a substantial increase in prices recently, but this story is unsatisfactory because why P rose "too high" is not explained.

The second states that P has not risen unreasonably, but for some reason M has flown the country. The NBG cites statistics that the stock of money in circulation in Georgia has fallen by nearly 50 percent in the last year. This is attributed to capital flight. Here again the reasoning lacks a key step: why (and to where) have the people of Georgia shipped their rubles? One possibility was that Georgians carry rubles in suitcases across the border into Turkey, obtaining the parallel exchange rate in their purchases of foreign goods for re-import into Georgia. But these rubles are worthless unless returned to the ruble zone; the majority of those leaving must recross the border into Georgia.[b] The only other channel for loss of rubles is through deficits in ruble-zone trade, and in 1991 trade statistics indicate a trade deficit of roughly 5 percent of GDP: large, but not large enough to cause the attributed fall in M given the increases in money supply that occurred simultaneously.

A third possibility suggested by policy-makers is that the velocity of money v has fallen. On its face, this is contradicted both in theory and in observation: theory suggests that v rises rather than falls as inflation rises, and observation in Kazakhstan and Georgia suggests that consumers recognize the ruble's loss in value and spend it for goods whenever possible. However, it is true that non-food consumer goods have become much more scarce in Georgia in recent months; this would argue for forced saving by consumers and a possible fall in v.

These explanations all have plausible features, but defects as well. Further, they do not provide an explanation for the difficulties producers have in obtaining cash (since they produce the goods that the available cash is spent upon), nor for the premium of cash for non-cash rubles.

---

[a] It is acceptable in these countries to identify currency with the money supply, for there is almost no reliance upon demand deposits or any other financial instrument for transactions purposes.

The Cash Shortage Phenomenon
(continued)

An alternative explanation of the "cash shortage" more consistent with these facts is that it is a manifestation of financial disintermediation. The shortage of currency begins with the financial system, and is epidemic only in those sectors reliant upon the organized financial markets for services. Savers are reluctant to place their currency in saving deposits; the financial system thus has few ruble notes when the government or producer draws down its account or takes out a loan for payroll or input purchase. The currency shortfall then leads to the real implications noted above. The shortfall is exacerbated by the fact that few of the producers in Georgia produce consumer goods; there are thus few purchases in currency of the producers' goods that would provide cash for deposit in the banking system. In terms of the quantity equation one can say that there are two sectors coexisting: the state sector for production of investment goods and a private (bazaar) sector for foodstuffs and other consumer goods. The banking system intermediates for the state sector, while there are only informal private intermediaries. M is used in both sectors. However, once it is spent in the state sector it flows in part into the private sector for bazaar transactions or non-bank saving.

The trends in the ratios of saving and time deposits to nominal net material product strongly suggest a process of disintermediation. The share of savings in NMP fell from 70.4 percent in end December 1990 to 6.9 percent by end May 1992 while the share of time deposits in NMP feel from 25 percent to 5.1 percent in the same period. Disintermediation is also suggested by the net outflow of cash from the banking system during the first 5 months of 1992 (Table 5.2, Statistical Appendix).

Savers may be reluctant to place their currency in saving deposits for two reasons. First, the interest rate offered on saving deposits and certificates (certificates of deposit) is negative in real terms: 4.5 percent in nominal terms in 1991, rising to roughly 12-25 percent in nominal terms in 1992. Given inflation of over 1000 percent in the last two years, the returns on such deposits are strongly negative. Given the shortage of consumer goods, however, the proper comparison may be with the return on holding currency -- which is even more negative in real terms. However, saving accounts are much less liquid than currency. Withdrawal rights have been limited in Kazakhstan for over a year, and in Georgia for most of 1992. This disparity in liquidity of savings deposits and cash has led to the phenomenon of premia on cash rubles over "non-cash" rubles.

This diagnosis has four immediate policy implications. First, the present policies to limit saving withdrawals only make the cash shortage worse. As they reduce the liquidity of bank deposits they increase the incentive toward disintermediation. Second, inflows of banknotes will not solve the problem. They will help the government to meet the payroll in the short run, but will disappear as well from the banking system almost immediately, circulating to purchase bazaar goods or going into the non-bank saving of consumers. Third, policies to make consumer goods available through organized market channels will serve directly to alleviate the cash shortage by encouraging their spending. Fourth, introduction of a credible financial instrument with sufficiently high interest rate will draw some of this currency back into the banking system, alleviating the cash shortage.

Note that the policies suggested in the third and fourth points will be anti-inflationary. More goods on the market will limit inflation, as will the reduction in demand implied by the increase in saving. Making consumer goods available may in the short run lead to budget and trade deficits. Successful introduction of the financial instrument will provide a means for non-inflationary financing of the budget deficit.

The four competing "cash shortage" hypotheses are in principle testable. The disintermediation hypothesis could be tested through making a stock of consumer goods available for cash at market prices. The proceeds would then enter the banking system. A strong demand response to this stock of goods would suggest that the rubles do in fact remain in country. Another possibility would be to initiate a small test marketing of a financial instrument with guaranteed positive interest rate but requires deposits in cash rubles. Significant response to the program would provide evidence that the ruble overhang continues coincident with disintermediation.

Endnotes

1.   The population in Georgia is about 1.9 percent of the population of the FSU, and its area roughly 0.3 percent of the total.

2.   This estimate is based on the World Bank's Atlas methodology. According to these estimates, Georgia's per capita income ranks 12th. out of the 15 independent republics of the FSU. Estonia had the highest per capita GNP ($3830) in 1991 and Tadjikistan the lowest ($1050).

3.   In 1989, agriculture's share in NMP in Georgia was 28 percent compared to 23 percent in the FSU.

4.   The ratio of total trade to GDP in 1988 in the larger republics of Russia, Ukraine, Kazakhstan and Belarus was 22 percent, 34 percent, 34 percent and 51 percent respectively. In the smaller republics of Azerbaijan, Lithuania, Moldova and Armenia the share of trade in GDP was 42 percent, 55 percent, 53 percent and 55 percent respectively.

5.   It was estimated, for example, that in 1990 one ruble worth of imports of oil and gas would cost as much as $2.5. The exchange rate was $1 to Rbl 0.6. Oil and gas imports constituted 16 percent of Georgia's total inter-republican imports in 1990. **Source:** David Tarr: Terms of Trade Effects on Countries of the former Soviet Union (August 1992).

6.   The correlation coefficient between the growth rate of GNP in Russia and Georgia during 1980-91 was about 70 percent. Of Georgia's total exports to the FSU, 67 percent went to Russia alone in 1991. More than 59 percent of Georgia's imports from the FSU came from Russia in 1991. Virtually all crude oil and oil products as well as natural gas were imported from Russia until 1992.

7.   For example, imports of natural gas were reduced from 5.5 billion cubic meters in 1990 to 4.6 billion cubic meters in 1991 due to the gas blockade caused by events in Ossetia. Imports of fuel oil from Russia feel from 2743 million tons in 1990 to 1652 million tons in 1991 and to only 300,000 million tons in 1992. In 1992, as a result of the severe cutback in imports of crude oil from Russia, production of gasoline in Georgia was reduced to only about 380,000 tons compared to a planned 3.5 million tons.

8.   Energy prices alone rose 50-100 times in 1991-92. See Annex 2.

9.   For instance, the production and processing of tea (Georgia's main export product) was particularly hurt by the continuing disturbance in Abkhazia where it is grown. In 1992, the production of tea was only about a third of the 1991 level.

10.   The picture was different in 1990, when the impact of the decline in real NMP on domestic availability was compensated in part by an increase in net imports.

11.   See Chapter 2 of Russia CEM (World Bank, September 1992). It was estimated that at the end of 1990, the overhang of excess wealth for households alone would imply a 50 percent price increase in the event of price liberalization.

12.   In 1991, the consolidated fiscal deficit of the FSU increased to 26 percent of GDP (as compared to a planned deficit of 5 percent) and Russia's own deficit soared to 31 percent of GDP. Credit flows from the monetary system to the Russian government financed 22 percent of GDP of the deficit. The rest of the gap was financed by transfers from enterprises. See Russia CEM (World Bank, September 1992).

13. The government budget includes the republican budget, the consolidated budgets of the local authorities and the operations of the Social Security Fund. This does not include scheduled interest payments on Georgia's share (1.6 percent) of FSU debt.

14. In fact, expenditures on the national economy (including various subsidies) and "other" expenditures rose in real terms, while the brunt of expenditure cuts fell on social and cultural activities, including health, education and welfare.

15. The previous government did not follow the lead of the other Soviet republics in raising many commodity prices in April 1991, so that price differentials were created favoring export of Georgian staples. Export restrictions were used through late 1991 and early 1992 to forestall such outflows of necessities. In 1992, liberalization of prices was implemented in Georgia later than in Russia (January 1), leading to still further strains on the ruble-zone trade and increasing budgetary subsidies.

16. Thus, at the end of 1990, the ratio of savings (time) deposits to NMP was 70.4 percent (25 percent). By end of 1991, the ratio was down to 60 percent (16 percent) and by end May 1992 it had fallen to 6.9 percent (5.1 percent). Including ruble issues, savings deposits and time and other deposits, the money supply increased by 43.5 percent between end 1990 and end 1991 and by 37.9 percent between December 1991 and May 1992. With prices rising by 123 percent between end 1990 and end 1991 and by more than 500 percent between December 1991 and May 1992, there was a significant real decline in money supply.

17. Thus revenues from VAT were only 3 percent of GDP compared to a planned 10 percent. This was due to the civil strife, but also reflected weakness in tax administration and lack of proper knowledge among taxpayers.

18. For example, existing excise taxes on alcohol and cigarettes were increased on July 25 and new excise taxes were introduced.

19. For example, the import price of liquid gas increased from Rbl 72 per ton in 1990 to Rbl 166 in 1991 and to Rbl 1200 in the first quarter of 1992. The import price for natural gas jumped from Rbl 42 per thousand cubic meters in 1990 to Rbl 51 in 1991 and to Rbl 1710 per thousand cubic meters in the first quarter of 1992. The price of crude oil increased from Rbl 90 per ton in end 1991 to Rbl 1000 per ton by May 1992. Imported electricity prices rose between 386 percent and 944 percent in the same period, depending on the source of supply (see also Annex 2).

20. Based on trade data for 1990, it has been estimated that if import and exports take place at world prices, Georgia's terms of trade with the rest of the former Soviet Union would deteriorate by almost 33 percent. While terms of trade with the rest of the world would improve at the same time (because Georgia would receive a better price for its exports of non-ferrous metals, some machinery, wood and paper, and some light industry), this improvement would not compensate for the deterioration in inter-republican terms of trade. Overall, terms of trade would deteriorate by about 19-20 percent. **Source: David Tarr, (August 1992).**

CHAPTER 2

Medium-Term Prospects

As described in the previous chapter, Georgia begins its transition to a market based economy under difficult economic conditions. Output has fallen sharply over the course of the last few years, inflation has reached unprecedented levels, and notwithstanding the underground economy, living standards of the population have deteriorated. What are the short and medium terms prospects for the economy, and what policies are necessary to exploit the economy's full potential?

This chapter outlines a highly stylized path for the Georgian economy, under the assumption that the government resolutely implements a comprehensive program of stabilization policies and structural reforms. This is a hazardous exercise even in the best of circumstances. In present conditions the scenario can only be indicative: even the short term outlook is very uncertain. What it suggests, however, is that with the right policies and institutions, and with adequate financial and technical support from the international community, Georgia has reasonably good medium term prospects. The prognosis of continuing recession in the neighboring region, and the economic and political uncertainty, will restrain quick recovery in the short term. However, with the improvement in the external environment in the medium term, and the establishment of market-based institutions, Georgia will be able to exploit its economic potential fully. Strong and sustained growth may be envisaged, with exports as the engine of growth.

A key to economic recovery is the implementation of a comprehensive program of reforms that combines stabilization policies and structural reforms. Appropriate macroeconomic stabilization policies, including tight fiscal and monetary policies, are essential to stabilize expectations and create the necessary confidence about the economy among investors, both domestic and foreign. And structural reforms are necessary to create a competitive market environment as well as the institutions and structures that encourage agents to respond to market forces. Indeed, as experience in other reforming economies has amply demonstrated, stabilization cannot be successful unless buttressed by structural reforms aimed at improving the mobilization and allocation of resources. And none of the structural reforms will induce the positive supply response if the economy slides into hyper-inflation or loses control of its external balances.

Economic recovery will also depend very much on adequate external financial flows. Without these flows, even with resolute implementation of reforms, the contraction in output and consumption would be too high and could jeopardize the efforts to create a market economy. In the short term, external financing will be necessary to finance imports that are essential to complement the limited and contracting domestic supplies of final consumption goods, as well as of inputs critical to production. It is also required to finance critical technical assistance in various aspects of economic policy making and implementation. External resources are necessary to help finance the upsurge in investment and imports that is necessary for growth in the medium term. In the near term, most of this financing must come from official sources. Thereafter, as the reforms take hold and there is evidence of macroeconomic stability, commercial external flows (including direct foreign investment) will play a greater role. To ensure that foreign technical and financial assistance is used most effectively, it will be important to coordinate and manage external assistance of various forms and from different sources.

Output, Consumption and Investment

The path of the economy is summarized in Table 2.1 and Figure 2.1. The prognosis of continuing contraction of the Russian economy in 1993, the disruption of trade, and the uncertain political and military situation within Georgia will prevent any significant reversal in the economic downturn experienced during 1990-92. Overall, real GDP could decline by as much as 15 percent during 1993, and by another 5 percent in 1994.

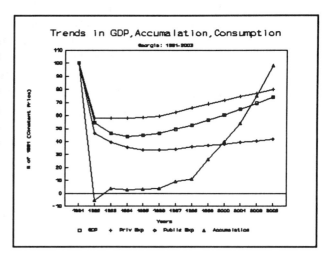

GEORGIA
Table 2.1
Trends in Macroeconomic Variables 1992-2003

	Actual 1991	Estimated 1992	Projected 1993-95	Projected 1996-2003
percent of GDP				
Consumption	88	91	107	100
-Private	75	80	97	92
-Public	13	11	10	8
Accumulation	11	-1	1	5
Losses on fixed capital	2	15	5	0
Resource Balance (+ =surplus)	0	-5	-13	-5
Imports (GNFS)	26	18	24	26
Exports (GNFS)	26	13	11	21
Real Growth Rates (%)				
GDP		-46	-6	7
Consumption		-44	-1	4
-Private		-42	0	4
-Public		-54	-10	3
Accumulation		-761	-4	58
Imports (GNFS)		-62	6	7
Exports (GNFS)		-72	3	10

There are at least two important reasons why a quick recovery in output is unlikely. First, as observed in Chapter 1, the Georgian and Russian economies are closely connected. While in the medium term this dependence may diminish as the economy re-orients itself to the world economy, the short term prospects of the Georgian economy will inevitably be tied closely to that of Russia. The prognosis of continuing collapse of output in Russia until 1995 means that further contraction of the Georgian economy is inevitable, at least till 1995. Second, experience in reforming east European economies has shown that, even with good implementation of economic reforms, recovery takes time. While output shrinks in the state sector, the increase in output in the newly emerging private sector is too small to compensate for this decline. In almost all the countries, the contraction of output continued at least for two years after reforms were initiated, and in all cases, the positive output response took longer to emerge than originally projected (Table 2.2).

GEORGIA
Table 2.2
GDP Growth in Central and Eastern European Countries
(1989-92)

	1989 Actual	1990 Actual	1991 Original Estimate	1991 Actual	1992 Original Estimate	1992 Latest Estimate
GDP at constant prices			*(Percent change)*			
- Bulgaria	0	-12	-11	-23	-4	-8 - -10
- Czechoslovakia	---	0	-5	-16	-5	-6 - -8
- Hungary	0	-4	-3	-11	2	-5
- Poland	0	-12	3	-7	0-1	1
- Romania	-6	-7	0	-13	-5	-15

A significant turn-around in economic activity can be expected after 1995, for several reasons. First, the recovery of the Russian economy will exert a strong influence on the Georgian economy, reflecting the magnifying impact observed in Chapter 1. To exploit this opportunity, policies to facilitate exports will be crucial. This will include maintaining tight control on domestic demand (primarily government consumption) and trade facilitating measures such as the elimination of export restrictions, provision of information to exporters etc. A clearing arrangement may also be helpful in facilitating inter-regional trade. Continued strong growth in exports is projected. Growth in domestic demand will come primarily from the private sector and from restructured small and medium enterprises, though presently these sources are relatively small components of total demand.

On the supply side, the implementation of stabilization policies to ensure macroeconomic stability, and structural reforms that increase the profitability of investments, should induce greater private sector investment. As a result, accumulation and net fixed investment are expected to increase strongly after 1995.[1] Newly privatized firms will demand new investment to compete in international markets, and investment will be necessary in the restructuring of remaining state enterprises as well. Economic policies to promote savings, and their efficient use for productive investments are therefore very important. These include for example, maintaining a stable currency, ensuring remunerative interest rates on savings, the introduction of new financial instruments, improved prudential regulations in banks, and appropriate training in banks and other financial institutions (see Chapter 5). Moreover, there is urgent need for public investment in critical infrastructure, especially transport and telecommunication, which has also been neglected in the last few years. These should be developed rapidly to support the growth of private sector investment. Initially, the agriculture sector and services will be the fastest growing sectors. In agriculture, it may be expected that the progressive privatization of land (80 percent by 1993) will generate substantial productivity gains; already private sector producers of all major agricultural crops have higher yields than state or cooperative producers (Tables 6.2-6.3, Statistical Appendix). Industry will also register positive growth, due to small and medium restructured state enterprises and the growth of new private ventures.

Already in 1990-92, private consumption is estimated to have declined by a cumulative 59 percent. Given the likely contraction in GDP, there will be no positive growth in private consumption in 1993. However, increased foreign borrowing will help avert further declines in private consumption, which grows by about 1 percent in 1995 and by 3-5 percent per year thereafter. Despite this growth, even at the end of the decade the level of private consumption recovers to only three quarters the level prevailing in 1991. Thus considerable belt-tightening and sacrifice from the population is required in the coming years.

External Trade Prospects

Imports

Just as the breakdown in trade with Russia in 1991-92 had a large adverse impact on Georgia's economy, a recovery of trade is likely to have a strong positive impact. Thus policies to facilitate trade with Russia and with the rest of the world will have a large pay-off.

After the precipitous decline in the volume of imports in 1991 and 1992,[2] a recovery in imports is critical for moderating the decline in output. Imports will also be necessary to augment domestic production and prevent continuing declines in private consumption. After declining slightly in 1993, imports are expected to increase by an average of 8-9 percent annually during 1994-95. They continue to grow strongly after 1995 (annual growth rate averaging 7 percent during 1995-2003), though the rate of growth slackens to a slower pace than export growth. The growth of imports is not unreasonable - severe import compressions can be expected to be followed by a quick recovery to previous levels.

Exports

Given Georgia's small size, exports to the FSU, and increasingly to the rest of the world, will provide the main demand side impetus to growth in the economy. Traditionally, Georgia's leading export sectors have been food industry (vegetables and fruit preserves, wine, tea, brandy, citrus), light industry (leather footwear, mineral water), machine building and metal-working (ferrous and non-ferrous metal). This structure may change as Russia and the rest of the FSU adopt an open trade regime with the rest of the world. Moreover, Georgian exporters will also be able to exploit their comparative advantage in trade with the rest of the world.[3] The sharp decline in exports in 1991 and 1992 is expected to continue in 1993. Thereafter, in response to the improved macroeconomic environment, restoration of trade and payments arrangement, and cessation of hostilities, exports are expected to grow strongly during 1994-95. Even with these increases, the volume of exports in 1995 is still only 30 percent of the level of exports in 1991. Thereafter, the growth in exports is projected at 10 percent annually between 1996-2003.

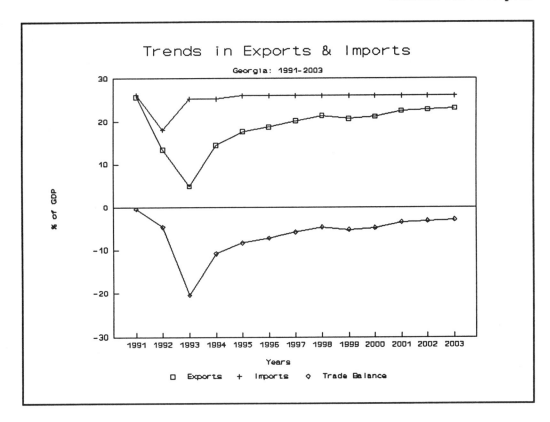

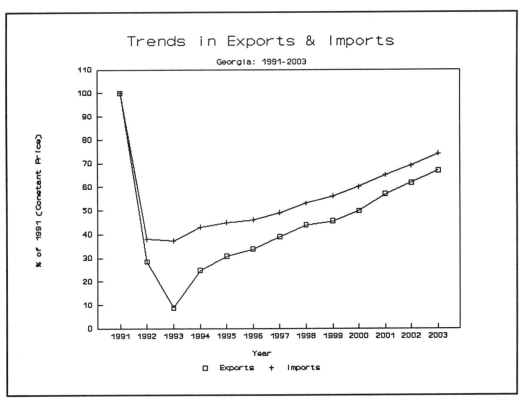

Figure 2.2

Achieving these results will depend very much on the implementation of appropriate policies and also on adjustment and restructuring in the productive branches. First and foremost, it will require maintaining tight fiscal and monetary policies. Restrictions on exports need to be lifted and appropriate incentives provided for exporters. Enterprises and entrepreneurs who so far have not had to bother exploring markets for their products need to be assisted by providing information on potential markets. They also need help in developing marketing skills. However, all these measures will not be enough. Fundamental changes in ownership and in the structure of enterprises are necessary to enable owners, managers and workers to respond to competition and to retain existing export markets and capture new ones (Chapter 5).

External Financing Needs

Despite strong growth in exports, and considerable belt-tightening, Georgia will require substantial external financial assistance to overcome the terms of trade shock and to lay the foundations for a sustained economic recovery. Given its falling income levels due to the disruptions in the traditional monetary, trade and transport systems and the civil conflicts in and around Georgia -- by the end of 1992 Georgia was among the poorest FSU republics -- it will be essential that this assistance contain a substantial degree of concessionality. If this assistance is not forthcoming, further compression in imports would be unavoidable. This would have an adverse impact on production and living standards, which have already fallen sharply in the past 2-3 years.

Georgia's annual financing requirements during 1993-95 are in the range of $250-$350 million (Table 2.3). These resources are largely required to finance a trade deficit in the range of $200 - $250 million. The rest goes towards some build up of reserves, and repayment of interest and amortization of new borrowings. This assumes that Georgia will be able to reschedule all principal and interest payments due on inherited ex-Soviet debt during 1993-95, or these liabilities will be taken over by Russia in exchange for Georgia's share of the inherited foreign assets of the FSU.[4]

All imports do not need to be paid for in foreign exchange. Indeed, in the short run, to the extent a large part of imports will be purchased from Russia and paid in rubles, the foreign exchange required to purchase the remaining imports will be correspondingly less. However, foreign exchange earned from exports will also be less -- a large part of Georgia's exports are likely to be sold for rubles to Russia or other countries of the FSU. Insofar as Russia does not allow the accumulation of trade deficits in rubles, and trade between Georgia and Russia is balanced, the financing gap remains unchanged.[5]

At least until 1995, Georgia will have to rely largely on official (multilateral and bilateral) sources for new money, in the form of loans with guarantees from export credit agencies, grants and loans from governments, and loans from the international financial institutions. For these resources on the most advantageous terms to be forthcoming, Georgia would have to continue implementing a credible program of stabilization and structural reform. Voluntary lending by commercial banks is expected to pick up after 1995 when macroeconomic stability is restored and fundamental and irreversible structural reforms are in place. Exposure of commercial banks increases after 1995, at the expense of official creditors. Direct foreign investment is also likely to be marginal till 1995. Thereafter, as foreign investors gain confidence in the stability and growth prospects of the Georgian economy, foreign investment will be more forthcoming.

In the early years, at least until 1995, a large share of external financing is likely to take the form of balance of payments support so as to finance critical imports and moderate the decline in production. Other urgent priorities are technical assistance in various areas, and the financing of critical infrastructure that have been neglected in the past and are crucial for Georgia's integration in the world economy.

Balance of payment support will be important in 1993-95 not only to arrest a further significant deterioration in living standards, but also to underpin the progressive liberalization of the economy and the additional demands this may place on foreign exchange (for example, as a result of the liberalization of imports). Provided the government implements a comprehensive program of stabilization and reform, IMF and World Bank financing for balance of payments could be forthcoming over the period 1993-95. After 1995, if macroeconomic stability is achieved and important structural reforms are in place, financial support from the World Bank would increasingly shift toward project investment needs.

GEORGIA
Table 2.3
Sources and Uses of Foreign Exchange
(US$ millions unless otherwise stated)

	1993	1994-5
Sources of Financing		
-Exports	48	432
-Direct Foreign Investment	—	—
Total	48	432
Uses of Financing		
-Imports	248	682
-Addition to Reserves	20	38
-Interest Payment	7	26
-Amortization Payments	0	45
Total Uses	275	791
Total External Financing Required	227	359

There are significant investment needs in developing and maintaining the basic infrastructure of production. Investment is especially needed in transport and telecommunications: the existing network is in poor condition and is not oriented to serve the more open orientation of the Georgian economy. The lack of this infrastructure could be a major constraint to private, including foreign investment. Financing from the World Bank could serve as an important catalyst for additional private investment in these activities: it will also provide a vehicle for implementing the necessary legal, regulatory, institutional and tariff reforms that may be required.

Georgia will need a lot of help in developing the institutions and capabilities that are necessary to manage the transition to a market economy. This is needed in the government and related agencies that must design and implement the reform program, such as the ministry of finance, the ministry of labor, the national bank, the privatization agency, the statistical office etc. It will equally be needed in enterprises and banks to enable them to respond efficiently to the changing environment. International assistance must be mobilized for these purposes, and the World Bank expects to play a leading role in this effort.

Creditworthiness

It is difficult to assess creditworthiness in view of the large uncertainties in the external environment, in the capacity to implement domestic economic policy reforms, and in the ability of the real economy to respond to changes in policy. With respect to the external environment, the major factor is the civil conflict. How quickly the situation can be normalized will have a critical impact on Georgia's growth and its capacity to earn foreign exchange. With respect to the latter, the potential for exports to the hard currency markets is still largely untested. Though Georgia has certain commodities (primarily agricultural and agro-industrial such as tea, citrus, wine, mineral water) and services (such as tourism) that have a good potential for earning hard currency, to what extent and at what speed other "soft" exports can be converted to "hard" goods for exports to the western markets is an open question. Georgia's export earnings will also depend on the trade policies of West European countries.

The extent of hard currency borrowing and its servicing will depend very much on the trade and payments arrangements that emerge between Georgia and the rest of the FSU, notably Russia. Insofar as a relatively larger share of imports can be financed through ruble credits from Russia, a larger share of Georgia's exports could be sold for hard currency. All indications are that the scope for such credits is extremely limited at best.

Even assuming that Georgia accepts the "zero option" and does not have to service any of the external debt undertaken by the FSU, the debt service burden on newly acquired debt will be high even in the most favorable scenario outlined above. In the early years, particularly in 1993, hard currency earnings from exports may be insufficient to service obligations on debt undertaken in 1992. Thereafter, a rapid increase in exports will help lower the debt service ratio though without concessionary finance it will continue to remain high throughout the decade. Given the uncertainty about export earnings, especially in the short term, external financing on concessionary terms will be required to ease the debt burden and facilitate the transition.

The Major Risks and Uncertainties

Georgia boasts a long tradition of entrepreneurship which has flourished despite enormous barriers. This provides it with a great advantage as reforms unshackle the economy from government control. Existing family ties provide a robust social safety net, which can cushion the impact of the transition even when the Government is not in a position to do so. Nevertheless, the transition is fraught with uncertainties and risks. Some of these can be addressed by Georgian policy-makers; however, others are beyond Georgia's control and the challenge will be to adjust to these shocks in an orderly way.

The most important uncertainty, and one which poses the biggest risk to the scenario of economic stabilization and recovery, is the normalization of the political situation. The longer normalization is delayed, the more the authority of the government will be undermined, making it all the more difficult to re-instill confidence that is necessary for the success of stabilization and the implementation of difficult reforms. The elections of mid-October 1992 resulted in the formation of a government with popular support. Hopefully it can initiate the comprehensive program of stabilization and reform on which economic recovery depends. Without this, one can expect the budget deficit to widen further as tax collection deteriorates with the authority of the government, there is increasing accumulation of arrears, and a breakdown of payment discipline. The consequence is hyper-inflation and widespread social dissatisfaction. Moreover, in this environment there will be no investment, and no hope for future recovery.

Among exogenous factors, an important down-side risk, at least in the short term, is that economic reforms in Russia are undermined and economic recovery and stability are not achieved there. Weak economic recovery in Russia would adversely affect Georgia in at least two ways. First, demand for Georgian products would diminish and the stimulus to export led growth weakened. Second,

Georgian producers may face a shortage of essential inputs that are produced in Russia, forcing cuts in domestic production. To cushion the impact of these developments, it is important that Georgia seek to diversify markets for its exports and imports. Autarkic tendencies should be resisted. Rather, opening of trade with the rest of the world should be encouraged. This will require not only policies to promote exports to the rest of the world, but also necessary investments in infrastructure, especially ports and telecommunications, that will improve Georgia's access to the rest of the world.

Georgia will have to guard against the risk of continuing macroeconomic instability in Russia. In this context, the government has rightly decided to introduce its own currency. To stabilize the currency, the government will have to strengthen its capacity to conduct an independent macroeconomic policy, and in particular strengthen the ability of the NBG and the Ministry of Finance to implement tight financial policies.

Another important exogenous factor that could adversely affect Georgia's economic recovery is the lack of adequate external financial assistance. As shown above (para. 15), even with the best of policies, Georgia will require $250-350 million per year during 1993-95. If this support is not available, either the growth of consumption would have to be moderated, or investment curtailed. Moderating the growth of private consumption will not be easy: even assuming the availability of foreign capital, the level of private consumption in year 2003 is still below the level achieved in 1991. Cutting it further could endanger support for the transition.[6] On the other hand, reducing investment even further will slow down economic recovery. Already, the path of recovery is not very strong: even in the year 2003 GDP is 30 percent below the level in 1991. Improvements in productivity alone will not be sufficient to promote growth. Indeed, successful economic restructuring requires investment in new plant and equipment, without which it will be difficult to compete in new markets and produce new goods.

Availability of external financing -- particularly concessional finance -- will depend on the favorable perception among international creditors about Georgia's economic prospects. This in turn depends very much on the implementation of appropriate economic policies by the government, along the lines recommended in this report. Measures to ensure macroeconomic stability, the creation of a stable legal and regulatory environment, and other policies to encourage the private sector will be crucial to attract foreign resources into Georgia.

Even if the external environment is good, there is the risk of poor implementation of economic policies by the government. This may happen either because the government does not have the political will to carry out the reforms, or because of inadequate implementation capacity and experience. One of the big policy risks is the government may find it difficult to cut back public expenditures even as revenues decline. Increasing recourse to money creation to finance the deficit could result in accelerating inflation and increasing tendencies towards the underground economy. This in turn will further undermine the government's ability to conduct economic policy, leading to economic instability. It is to minimize these risks that the report gives such importance to measures to strengthen tax collection and widen the revenue base. Another policy risk is the government falters in implementing systemic reforms, particularly the restructuring and privatization of state enterprises. Experience elsewhere has shown that in the absence of a hard budget constraint, and without changes in the ownership structure and in governance of state enterprises, prospects for economic recovery can be considerably delayed. It is thus important for the government to stop bailing out unprofitable activities and to emphasize speed and simplicity in designing reforms to restructure and/or privatize enterprises.

The lack of adequate institutional capacity, and experience and skills within the government to design and implement reforms is another constraint on the speed of recovery. So is the behavior of managers and workers in enterprises and banks, who have so far been shielded from responsibility and accountability. How quickly these institutions and attitudes can be transformed, and new institutions created to fulfill the needs of a market economy is a critical constraint to the speed of transition. There is little experience to go by, hence the uncertainty. Whatever experience there is suggests that without developing the right institutions as quickly as possible, a positive supply response will not be generated. Technical assistance must be mobilized to strengthen government's capacities in the critical areas of stabilization and reform. These would include most importantly strengthening the National Bank's capacity to maintain tight credit policies and to regulate and supervise commercial banks; the Ministry of Finance's capacity to collect taxes and to monitor and control spending; the Ministry of Social Welfare's ability to monitor the population in poverty and to design a tight social safety net for them; and the agencies responsible for restructuring and privatization of state enterprises, to help them implement a rapid program of privatization of small enterprises and to identify medium and large enterprises for restructuring and/or privatization.

Even with the best of outside technical assistance, there is only that much which can be accomplished in the next 1-2 years: institutional capacity constraints will remain. It is important to design reforms that take account of these limitations, and to focus on those areas that are most important for achieving a positive supply response and maintaining the momentum of reforms. Otherwise, existing capacities will be dispersed too thinly and very little will be achieved. The chapters that follow focus on the key tasks that must be accomplished to generate economic recovery and sustain the transition to a market economy. These include: (i) creating a stable macroeconomic environment; (ii) intensifying competition; (iii) enabling enterprises and banks (and owners, managers and workers) to respond to competition; and (iv) developing a social safety net that can cushion the impact of the reforms on the most poor without undermining fiscal responsibility and economic efficiency.

Endnotes

1. Over the period 1987-92 the share of accumulation in NMP fell from 20.6 percent to -1 percent; the share of net fixed investment in NMP fell from 14 percent to -1.6 percent. Both these trends are expected to be reversed.

2. In 1991, the value of total imports (in current rubles) fell by more than 21 percent, while imports from the ruble area fell 8 percent. With an inflation rate of 80-100 percent, this implies a huge real contraction. In 1992, the decline is even more severe. The value of total imports (in current rubles) rose 308 percent, when inflation exceeded 913 percent.

3. It is difficult to predict how the pattern of exports will change under a more open trade regime. One clue is provided by the calculations of relative price ratios for important exported product categories. These ratios, which estimate the dollar value of a ruble worth of exports, provide an indication whether the shift to world prices would be beneficial to the exporter or not. Based on 1990 trade figures, and foreign trade prices provided by GOSKOMSTAT, it appears that exports of oil and gas, ferrous and non-ferrous metals, machinery, wood and paper, and some other products would remain profitable under the new regime. Surprisingly though, agricultural exports do not do well in this comparison. Source: David Tarr (1992).

4. At the time of writing, Georgia was leaning towards accepting the so called 'zero option', in which Russia would take responsibility for servicing Georgia's share of FSU debt in return for Georgia relinquishing its claims on FSU assets.

5. Thus, it is reported that in trade negotiations between Georgian and Russian authorities, Georgian proposals for exports to Russia and considerably larger imports from Russia in the first quarter of 1993 were cut down by the Russian side to ensure balanced trade.

6. Thus if only half of the assumed foreign exchange was available, and all the adjustment was made in private consumption, the level of private consumption in 1995 would have fallen by as much as 44 percent compared to 1991.

CHAPTER 3

Policies for Macroeconomic Stabilization and Growth

The restoration of macroeconomic stability must remain a central objective of economic policy: without it no investment will occur and no growth can be sustained. The reduction of macroeconomic imbalances requires policies in the area of domestic demand management. But a comprehensive policy framework must integrate these stabilization measures with those designed to achieve greater efficiency in resource allocation and to minimize the contractionary effects on output of demand management policies. These policies must also support the medium term goals of increased market orientation and integration in the international economy.

STABILIZATION POLICIES

As long as Georgia remained in the ruble zone, it had only limited control over inflation. This was largely dependent on the fiscal policies of the Russian Government and the monetary policies of the Central Bank of Russia (CBR).[1] Maintaining the ruble as the medium of exchange made sense thus far. First, there was no real option: it was prudent to put off introducing a new currency until the government had the capacity to implement strict fiscal and monetary policies. Otherwise confidence in the new currency would be quickly undermined. Second, it made sense to wait and see whether there was a possibility of stabilizing the ruble in the context of the ruble area. A common and stable currency would minimize uncertainty, and thus facilitate inter-regional trade and moderate the decline in economic activity.

The latter half of 1992 and early 1993 saw a continuing decline in the value of the ruble and increasing difficulty in implementing a common ruble zone agreement. Georgia complained that Russia was strangling its economy by restricting the supply of rubles and foreign exchange; in turn, Russia accused the republics of trying to undermine stabilization by dumping rubles in exchange for goods and foreign exchange. In these circumstances, the advantages to trade by maintaining a common currency were overwhelmed by the disadvantages of uncertainty in the value of payments. Consequently, in early 1993 the government decided to introduce its own currency (the Lari). As a first step, coupons were issued in April 1993 and the new currency is expected to be in circulation by end 1993.

Having a new currency per se does not guarantee price stability (or even insulation from trends in Russia). That will require implementation of tight fiscal and monetary policies (as discussed below). And Georgia's exchange rate policy will determine how insulated prices in Georgia are with respect to those in Russia. Moreover, the introduction of a separate currency will entail short term costs in the form of further disruption in inter-regional trade. The new currency will be unknown, and confidence in holding it will have to be developed. With the right policies, this will develop over time, but in the short term trade disruption may be unavoidable.

There could be various options for Georgia's exchange rate policy. Fixing the rate with respect to a hard currency such as the German mark (at a substantially depreciated rate compared to the present ruble/mark rate) is one option. This has the advantage that to the extent Georgia is successful in maintaining the fixed rate, the Lari is likely to become the preferred currency for trade with Russia as well, and thus inter-regional trade will be facilitated. However, a credible fixed exchange rate policy requires the availability of adequate international reserves, which Georgia does not possess. Moreover, insofar as inflation in Georgia exceeds that in the other country, as is likely if Georgia progressively eliminates various subsidies, a fixed rate may reduce the incentives to export which is not desirable. In the circumstances, a floating exchange rate regime is preferable. It does not require a sizeable stock of international reserves and export competitiveness can be maintained in the face of adverse terms of trade shocks and other domestic price adjustments. However, there is the risk that the small number of transactions between the other currencies and the Lari would result in large fluctuations in the exchange rate, discouraging trade. A "crawling peg" with a commitment to maintaining export competitiveness may also make good sense in these conditions. In all circumstances, a tight fiscal and monetary policy is crucial to instill confidence in the value of the new currency.

Fiscal Policy

Tight fiscal policies will be necessary in the next few years. In 1992, the state budget deficit was approximately 35 percent of GDP. This level is similar to that found in many countries experiencing very high rates of inflation. As experience in other countries has demonstrated, a sharp reduction in the budget deficit is the common characteristic of successful stabilization episodes. Conversely, there are few cases where stabilization was achieved without a significant improvement in the fiscal balance.[2] A major policy objective of the Georgian government must be to balance the budget in the medium term, starting with a significant initial reduction in 1993.

The goal of reducing the budget deficit is made difficult by the very process of the transition the economy is undergoing. On the one hand, tax revenues are likely to shrink in the short term. The contraction in markets abroad, the disruption in trade, and the realignment of relative prices continue to drive unprofitable activities, mostly in state enterprises, out of business. Moreover, until new tax systems are in place, and tax administration sufficiently strengthened, private sector activities largely escape the taxation net. On the other hand, this very process of transformation increases claims on government resources. For example, the social safety net needs to be strengthened to cushion transitional hardships (e.g., increasing unemployment); public investment must be increased to rebuild dilapidated infrastructure inherited from the past; and at least some of the cost of cleaning up commercial banks' portfolio may have to be absorbed by the budget. Unless fundamental changes are introduced in public finance policies, fiscal imbalances could deteriorate even further. These changes must not only aim at widening the revenue base. All but the most important public expenditures (which would likely be confined to essential social programs and rehabilitation of critical infrastructure) will have to be cut. This will be a difficult political task.

Tax Policies and Administration

Georgia introduced a personal income tax and an enterprise profits tax effective January 1, 1992. A value added tax (VAT) and excise taxes were introduced effective March 1, 1992. These new taxes, which aim at broadening the revenue base - by including personal incomes and expenditures -- are in the right direction and contain the basic features found in the tax systems of market economies, including reasonable top rates for the taxes on income (40 percent) and profits (35 percent),[3] and a single rate of 14 percent for the VAT.[4] However, there remain serious deficiencies in the existing laws, including differentiation of rates of taxation by types of enterprise or source of income,[5] lack of clear depreciation rules, and the pervasiveness of exemptions that threaten the integrity of the tax base.[6] The IMF has made several recommendations to overcome these problems, including increases in excise taxes, the application of the VAT to all imports, a significant but temporary increase in the tariffs on imports from the non-ruble area, and the elimination of various tax exemptions and discounts (Box 3.1). Some of the recommendations have already been implemented and the others should be implemented as well.[7]

Considerable strengthening of tax administration is also urgently necessary, especially to cover private business activity (including that which is currently underground) that is likely to be the main growth sector in the future. The tax service will also have to take over that part of the tax collection that so far has been done automatically by the state banks. In addition, new processes, such as taxpayer registration, withholding at source, self assessment, enhanced collection procedures and audit will need to be developed, some from scratch. Extensive computerization as well as technical assistance will be required over the next few years.

Even with the best of tax systems, it has been the experience in most of the East European economies that it can take several years for new taxes to yield fully. In economies where tax administration systems need to be built up from scratch, there will be delays and initial shortfalls in receipt.[8] The scope for taxes, such as the personal income tax, to tap new revenue bases, notably in the emerging private sector, may remain limited for some time. Given these difficulties in strengthening the revenue base, expenditure reduction policies become crucial. The two main sources that can provide additional savings are subsidies and other transfers, and payments for social security. The scope for cuts in the public investment program appears to be limited.[9]

Expenditure Control

Subsidies and transfers accounted for about 21 percent of total expenditures of the state budget (and 10 percent of GDP) in 1992. These include subsidies for basic consumer goods and municipal services, such as food (bread, milk and meat), natural gas, heating, electricity, transportation and culture[10]. Further implicit subsidies also apply to other goods and services, such as domestic rents. These payments may be significantly reduced through targeting of benefits to those who are poor. Part of the savings so generated could be used to strengthen the safety net.

In 1992, the government planned to distribute about 12-13 percent of GDP in social security payments for unemployment compensation, pensions and other cash allowances. Given present trends in revenue and the increasing commitments due to rising unemployment[11] and falling living standards, existing programs would have to be reformed to ensure that these are affordable. This will require a combination of improved targeting of benefits to those that are poor, old age pensioners, unemployed, or with large families, and some reduction in the level of certain type of benefits (pensions for working persons, expenditures on health camps, sports facilities etc, the maximum level of unemployment compensation). Specific proposals for reform of the pension system, family allowances, and unemployment compensation are discussed in Chapter 6.

Box 3.1		
Summary of Recommendations on Tax Policy		

Recommendation	Time Frame for Implementation	Fiscal Impact (Revenue effect)
1. Profit Tax		
Introduce equal treatment for determining the tax base for all taxable entities.	Next fiscal year	Strongly positive
Apply a single rate of 35 percent	Next fiscal year	Strongly positive
Limit exemption and tax holidays	Next fiscal year	Positive
Generalize compensation for losses	Next fiscal year	Clearly negative
Generalize deductions for interest payments	Next fiscal year	Probably negative
Establish detailed regulations for depreciation allowances	Immediate	Probably positive
2. Personal Income Tax		
Prepare for global income tax, while preserving the withholding at source system	Medium term	Strongly positive
As a first step remove the sharp differences in the present different schedules	Next fiscal year	Probably negative
Review and limit exemptions	Next fiscal year	Positive
Review and limit tax reductions	Next fiscal year	Positive
Apply a flat dependent allowance instead of proportional rates	Immediate	Positive
Introduce a presumptive minimum taxation of small businesses	Immediate	Strongly positive
3. VAT		
Introduce VAT exemption threshold	Immediate	Neutral
Generalize the invoice system and abolish the margin-based VAT	Immediate	Strongly positive
Review and limit exemptions in particular for services	Immediate	Positive
Allow for VAT deduction for capital goods	Immediate	Strongly positive
4. Excises		
Increase some rates of taxation	Immediate	Strongly positive
Introduce some excises	Immediate	Strongly positive
5. Taxation of imports		
Apply VAT on imports from outside CIS	Immediate	Strongly positive
Apply excises on imports from outside CIS	Immediate	Strongly positive
Increase the rate of the import duty	Immediate	Strongly positive

Source: Georgia: Basic Issues in Taxation, Budgetary and Social Expenditure Policy for an Economy in Transition, IMF (August 1992)

Financing the Deficit

Even under the most optimistic scenario, it is unlikely that the tax and other revenues will be adequate to meet all claims on government resources in the near term. Deficit financing will be inevitable. However, as long as Georgia is in the ruble zone, it cannot resort to money creation to finance its deficit. Even when Georgia issues its own currency, use of money creation to finance the deficit would be inflationary and would cause loss of international confidence in the new currency at a time when such confidence is vital to economic recovery. Recourse to this kind of financing should be limited.

As discussed earlier, increasingly the deficit is being financed through credit creation and by accumulation of arrears. Both these methods are costly: the first because it will tend to reduce the competitiveness of Georgian products; the second because it will undermine payment discipline and encourage entrepreneurs to flee the official economy, further eroding the tax base.

As much as possible, government bonds issued directly to the public should be considered as a means for financing the budget deficit. If offered competitive interest rates, these would provide a non-inflationary source of financing, as well as a means to forestall financial disintermediation. It would provide an impetus for a secondary market in those bonds that could serve to widen domestic financial markets and promote savings, an important objective of macroeconomic policy.

Monetary and Credit Policy

Tight credit policies will be required in the next few years to avoid inflationary pressures. Expectations of cheap and excessive credit to enterprises would encourage inventory accumulation and currency substitution, further worsening macroeconomic imbalances. Tight ceilings on credits to the public sector, including state enterprises, should be implemented. To increase the cost of credit, the NBG should consider increasing interest rates on refinancing credits (currently 40 percent) to the level charged by the CBR.[12] This policy would also encourage commercial banks to attract savings from the population and force interest rates up to more remunerative levels. As already mentioned in Chapter 1, increasing interest rates is important to promote financial savings and financial intermediation. It is also crucial to overcome the cash shortage that Georgia is currently experiencing.

Incomes Policy

Given the lack of effective ownership within state enterprises, and consequently the absence of a countervailing influence to balance the wage demand of workers, there is a risk that increases in wages will outstrip growth in labor productivity and weaken the competitiveness of production. Notwithstanding the negative impact of these policies on incentives, it will be essential in the short term to adopt some kind of explicit incomes policy for state enterprises (especially those that are not yet corporatized) to prevent excessive wage increases.[13] The policy may be relinquished once financial discipline has been established (or when substantial privatization has been completed).

Endnotes

1.   Of course, in a properly functioning ruble zone, these policies would have reflected the views of all the participants of the ruble zone. In fact, until now, non-Russian participants have complained that the policies largely reflect Russia's dominant position in the region.

2.   For example, the successful stabilization program in Israel in 1985 involved cutting the budget deficit from 10.4 percent of GNP in 1984 (when the inflation rate was 374 percent) to a surplus of 1.9 percent by 1986 (when the inflation rate was down to 48 percent). In Bolivia the deficit was 10.8 percent of GNP in 1985 (when the inflation rate was 117509 percent). The stabilization program successfully reduced inflation to 16 percent by 1988, when the deficit was 7.5 percent of GDP. Conversely, Argentina's failed stabilization during 1984-89 was largely because fiscal policy never decisively changed: the budget deficit was reduced from 11.2 percent of GNP in 1984 (inflation 627 percent) to 5.6 percent in 1986 (inflation 90 percent) but the deficit rose to 10.3 percent of GNP in 1989 (and inflation to 3079 percent). Source: Dornbusch Starzeger, and Wolf: Extreme Inflation: Dynamics and Stabilization (1990). Massive budget deficits also characterized the German hyperinflation of 1923, as well as that in Austria (1921-22) and Poland (1923). In these cases as well, successful stabilization required reducing the deficit significantly. Source: Dornbusch and Fisher: Stopping Hyperinflations Past and Present (1986).

3.   This applies to state enterprises (that is, one where state-owned capital is more than 50 percent of total). The tax rate for private enterprises is 30 percent, and for commercial banks 45 percent.

4.   The VAT rate was reduced from 28 percent to 14 percent in August 1992.

5.   For example, the enterprise profit tax distinguishes income from production process (profits) and income earned in financial transactions and other accessory activities (income).

6.   For example, there are 29 exemptions listed in the personal income tax law, including pensions, wages paid in foreign currency to citizens working abroad, a variety of fringe benefits, income from the sale of products from small holdings, and amounts used to purchase shares of state enterprises. In addition to the exemptions the law also provides for further deduction and tax preferences for such categories as small farming activities, members of collective farms, military and security personnel and invalids. The enterprise profit tax also contains several exemptions.

7.   For example, in early February 1993, excises and VAT were imposed on non-ruble area imports.

8.   This has already happened in Georgia. Between January-May 1992, total revenues were only 39 percent of the planned amount. Revenues from the VAT, which was projected to be the single most important source of revenues, were only 8 percent of the planned amount. In the first 11 months of 1992, the shortfall in VAT revenues was Rbl 2.1 billion and in profit taxes Rbl 134 million (see also Table 4.1, Statistical Appendix). For an interesting review of recent experience in East European economies, see Review of Experience with Programs in Eastern Europe: IMF (June 30, 1992).

9.   Already capital investment has been cut sharply: in 1991 capital investment in real terms was only 39 percent of the peak level in 1988. The public investment program for 1992 was also cut to the bone: of the total budgeted amount of Rbl 6.5 billion, Rbl 2.5 billion was allocated to the rehabilitation of areas damaged by natural disasters (earthquake, floods) and the battle in Tbilisi. Of the remaining Rbl 4 billion, investment in health, education (hospital and school construction etc) and communal services was almost Rbl 1.3 billion, highway and housing construction another 0.65 billion, Tbilisi subway 0.3 billion, and investment in electric power 0.4 billion. However, about 0.5 billion was allocated to agroindustry, and

another 0.3 billion to other branches and enterprises. These latter investments need to be carefully scrutinized and reduced if possible (see Table 4.3, Statistical Appendix).

10.   Subsidies for bread and electricity alone accounted for a quarter of total budgeted expenditures in the first quarter of 1993.

11.   Between January - December 1992, the number of unemployed rose 600 percent to 116,000 persons (5.4 percent of labor force). However, only 10.5 percent of these received financial assistance from the state. If structural reforms really take hold, and unemployment rises as it did in Poland, Czechoslovakia or Slovakia in the first two years of the stabilization program, the unemployment rate could rise to at least 7-8 percent in the first year. And the proportion of unemployed eligible for assistance from the state will also be much higher. See Chapter 6.

12.   Significant differences in interest rates in Georgia and elsewhere (notably Russia) could lead to capital flight. In 1992, the interest rates charged by the NBG for refinance credits lagged behind the rates set by the CBR. While the CBR rate was increased from 50 percent to 80 percent in May 1992, in Georgia the rate was still 50 percent as of June 1992 (later lowered to 40 percent). The relatively low interest rates on savings in Georgia may partly explain the disintermediation underway: between January-May 1992, there was a net outflow of cash from the banking system of Rbl 2.3 billion compared to a net inflow of Rbl 86 million in the same period of 1991 (Table 5.2, Statistical Appendix). Some of this outflow may represent capital flight out of the country (see also Box 1.2).

13.   Typically, this policy is implemented by imposing a prohibitive tax on wages above a certain norm determined according to projected changes in labor productivity.

PART II

THE AGENDA FOR STRUCTURAL REFORMS

Restoration of macroeconomic stability must remain a priority of government policy, and the measures outlined above are essential to achieve this objective. However, by themselves these will not be sufficient. They must be supported by structural reforms designed to increase the efficiency of resource use and to achieve the long term goal of establishing a market economy. These reforms include first, measures to progressively liberalize markets for goods and factors of production and so reduce government interventions in resource allocation (Chapter 4). Continued government intervention in setting prices and profit margins, controlling imports, directing credits, etc. distort market signals and lead to the mis-allocation of resources. They also inhibit the growth of the private sector. Second, systemic reforms are required to encourage and enable enterprises, banks and households to respond flexibly and efficiently to market signals and opportunities. Changes in the ownership and management structure in enterprises and banks is a key aspect of these reforms (Chapter 5). In their absence, there is no assurance that agents will not react perversely to market signals. And finally, it is necessary to provide an affordable social safety net for those that are poor and for those hurt by the transition (Chapter 6). For if these measures are not in place, the sustainability of reforms could be jeopardized. These three broad areas constitute the agenda for reform. The following chapters address each of these issues and identify concrete measures that could be implemented in the short and medium term.

As will be seen, the task is enormous. Yet, as in the other countries of the FSU, the capacity to design and implement reforms is limited. Even with the best of technical assistance and training, the pace and breadth of reforms will be constrained by the absorptive capacity of implementing agencies. Thus it is important to define priorities clearly, and to design reforms that are relatively easy to implement. At this stage, simplicity in design should take precedence over complicated and sophisticated approaches.

A second criteria for choosing priorities must be whether or not (and how seriously) the proposed reform strengthens or weakens the fiscal balance. As argued earlier, achieving macroeconomic stability is critical and the reduction of fiscal imbalances is a key to achieving this objective. Reforms that increase tax revenues or reduce claims on government resources should have priority over those that do the opposite, at least in the short term.

A third criteria should be whether or not the reforms seek to harnass the latent entrepreneurial talent of the Georgian people. As discussed in Chapter 1, there is some evidence suggesting the likelihood of considerable, and thriving, unreported economic activity. Bringing this sector into the mainstream of economic activity, and fostering its growth, is likely to have a strong ripple effect throughout the economy. Policies that promote this end, including in particular measures that reduce government intervention in economic activity, should be accorded priority.

Before outlining the priorities for economic reform, it is important to discuss two aspects that are extremely relevant for the success of economic reforms. The first is the necessity of transforming public administration to a state administration geared to the promotion and regulation of market relations. The second is to develop enforceable laws and regulations that provide the orderliness and predictability vital to the effective functioning of market relations.

Administrative reform has several dimensions. It includes defining the structure of the central government, the power and responsibilities of ministries, and the role of the civil service. It involves the re-organization of ministries so that they can be responsible for sectoral policy-making, promotion of economic and technical services to their sectors on a market-driven basis, and economic regulation rather than direct command and intervention. Adequate capacity to perform these functions must be developed. A critical aspect of administrative reform is the development of capacities in the core institutions and functions of economic management. This particularly affects the Ministries of Finance, Economy, External Economic Relations, Labor and Welfare and the National Bank, as well as several other agencies with the mandate to design and implement systemic reforms (such as the State Committee on Privatization). Administrative capacity is presently weak in precisely those areas vital to sound economic governance in a market economy: these include fiscal policy; government budgeting and the control of public expenditure; public accounting; supervision of the financial system and the control of credit; management of essential social programs (unemployment and poverty alleviation); and management of the country's external finances, including debt. In addition, there is a need to strengthen the statistical agencies, especially to cover the emerging private sector as well as the poor.

Not surprisingly, the legal framework for reform has not changed in step with the rapid pace of recent political and social changes. As a result, the old framework established by Soviet laws continues to exist, causing confusion and uncertainty in the minds of economic agents, domestic and foreign. New legislation on creation and transfer of property rights and on contract law, and their enforcement will form the cornerstones of enterprise reform, privatization and foreign direct investment. These need to be quickly adopted. However, legislation by itself will not be enough. The whole infrastructure of the judicial system will have to be developed over time to enforce the new laws and regulations consistent with a market based economy.

CHAPTER 4

Reforms to Enlarge the Role of Markets and Intensify Competition

Domestic Pricing and Trade

All prices were regulated by the state until the beginning of 1992, although there were parallel, or bazaar markets for many goods. As a first step in liberalizing markets, prices for a large number of commodities were liberalized in February 1992. Except for about 18-20 goods and services prices for all other commodities were freed of government intervention. A second round of liberalization was implemented on July 1, 1992: consequently, only prices of bread, milk (not milk products), medicines, housing rent, heating services, water and sewerage, coal, natural gas, liquid gas, electricity (for private and commercial users), passenger transport fares (for taxis and subway) and communications remain subject to government control. Very correctly, the government also moved to remove barriers to participation in commodity markets. Thus in May 1992 a decree was adopted allowing unrestricted trade among citizens. This decree applies to street and other informal trade.

Prices that were not liberalized have been increased several fold since January 1992 (Table 8.4, Statistical Appendix). Thus the price of bread was almost 14 times more in July than it was in January 1992 and in January 1993 it was up another 600 percent; meat prices tripled between January and July 1992, before they were liberalized. Milk prices in July were 7 times what they were in January 1992. And prices for other commodities in July were 30-40 times more than in January. These prices increases have significantly increased the cost of living of the population.

Given Georgia's extreme dependence on energy imports, and high energy intensity (Annex 2), pricing of energy products is particularly important. Unlike most other countries of the FSU, Georgia liberalized prices of several energy products, including gasoline, diesel oil and crude oil. Prices of other energy products that remain subject to government control were increased very sharply, reflecting the large increase in their import price.[1] The price of diesel fuel in July 1992 was 200 times higher than in January; crude oil prices 46 times higher; industrial fuel 100 times; natural gas 311 times; electricity for industrial users 40 times higher; and liquid gas 36 times higher.

Despite these adjustment in domestic energy prices, energy related subsidies constitute a large share of the total budgetary expenditures.[2] Moreover, imported energy prices are still below international prices and further increases in these prices are inevitable. For example, until mid 1992 crude oil was imported from Russia at a price between Rbl 4000-9000 per ton. At a world price of $120-150 per ton, import prices for crude oil were still no more than 50 percent of the international prices (at the exchange rate of Rbl 150 per dollar prevailing at that time). Similarly, the import price of natural gas (Rbl 1710 per '000 cubic meters) was only 11 percent of the international prices ($100 per '000 cubic meter). Further increases in energy prices will be required as import prices rise to international levels over the next few years.

To further expand the role of markets, prices of internationally traded energy products, such as coal and industrial fuel, should be liberalized. Till that time, their prices should be increased to fully reflect import, transportation and distribution costs. Prices for electricity and natural gas should also be set as above to at least cover their import price and transport and distribution costs. These measures will not only reduce budgetary subsidies and hence improve the fiscal balance. They will also encourage a more economical use of energy and thereby improve the external balance.

While prices have been largely liberalized and there are in principle no restrictions on trade, competition is still very limited. Moreover, existing ownership and managerial structures in state enterprises are such that enterprises are not motivated to generate profits for the owners. This has led to peculiar problems and to concerns about the emergence of middlemen (or "parasites" as some call them) who make profits by marking up prices because of existing scarcities.[3] The government sought to restrict such activities by limiting the mark-up, but that only led to a proliferation of middlemen.[4] The appropriate solution to these problems in the short term is to encourage competition, for example by having a state-supervised policy of soliciting competitive bids for the distribution of commodities to markets, and by eliminating barriers to imports if any. In the medium term, the privatization of state enterprises and new entry of private firms should succeed in eliminating the scarcity rent from these activities.

Another transitional problem is the extreme speculative mark-up of prices in the bazaar. For the short run, the model of the "Central Soyuz" cooperative marketing program for sugar may provide an alternative to both price controls and speculative excesses. This program operates without government subsidy to provide sugar at moderate prices to consumers. It has a rationing component that should not be necessary, but acts in the short run to dampen the speculative price increases in the bazaar.[5]

International Trade Regime

For a small economy like Georgia, international trade (including trade with countries of the FSU) provides a potent stimulus for competition. Imports provide competition to domestic producers in the home market, while Georgian exporters must compete with exporters from other countries in foreign markets. Competition through open international trade is particularly important in Georgia where the small size of the domestic market and the concentration of industry (common to all republics of FSU) precludes competition among a large number of domestic producers.

The existing trading system continues to be hampered by significant impediments to trade, especially various restrictions of exports for convertible currency and excessive regulation of trade among countries of the FSU. As discussed in Chapter 2, the prospects for economic recovery in Georgia depend strongly on its success in promoting exports. Restrictions on exports will only slow down economic growth. The disruption in inter-regional trade has already caused a significant drop in production: too abrupt a disruption of existing production and trade patterns could endanger the transformation process. Measures to facilitate inter-regional trade will be required to arrest this tendency and to ease the transition.

With respect to the import regime, Georgia is ahead of most other countries of the FSU. Imports from the countries of the FSU are completely free and neither tariffs nor quantitative restrictions apply. There are virtually no tariffs (only a 2 percent custom duty) or import quotas in trade with other countries. Thus, provided the importer has acceptable means of payment -- rubles, dollars, or other goods -- there are no restrictions on imports from any part of the world. This is the right policy stance. It should be maintained even when there is increasing pressure on the government from enterprises to shield them from competition by erecting barriers to imports either in the form of high tariffs or import quotas. If some temporary protection is found to be unavoidable, a uniform import tariff of around 15 percent may be applied.

While the import regime is liberal, effective competition from imports from third countries is limited. This is because imports are too expensive at the current exchange rate: at the current exchange rate, the purchasing power of the dollar in Georgia is much higher than abroad.[6] This condition cannot be sustained indefinitely: either domestic prices will rise or the domestic currency will appreciate against the dollar to approximately equalize the purchasing power of the dollar abroad and in Georgia. Effective competition from imports will intensify.

Competition from imports is also hindered indirectly by the restraints on exports (see below). Quantitative restrictions on exports (in the form of licenses) will inhibit exports and the reduced foreign exchange inflows will make imports more inaccessible.[7] As these export restrictions are eliminated, and the currency appreciates, import competition should further increase.

In contrast to the import regime which is relatively free, restrictions on exports are pervasive.[8] These restrictions mostly take the form of export licensing, which applies to inter-regional trade as well as trade with other countries. Exports of 12 items (milk and dairy products, live animals, food products, wheat, flour, building materials, wood, leather, sugar, oil and calcium soda) are currently banned. In addition, there is a list of 40 items that require export license.[9]

There are no plausible reasons to maintain the pervasive system of export licensing (with one exception, see Box 4.1). At a time when the exchange rate provides a strong incentive to export, these licenses discourage exporters. Given the prognosis of the continuing need to restrain domestic demand, and the likely recession in the region for the next few years, it is important to exploit every opportunity to export. The export licensing system should be significantly scaled back. Licensing for exports to the convertible currency area should be eliminated. And for exports to the countries of the FSU, those that are based on barter should not be restricted.

In the circumstances now prevailing, the payments arrangements between republics are working poorly. There is a continuing dependence upon barter and state trading arrangements. Enterprise to enterprise transactions across republican borders are difficult because deposit rubles in one republic are not always convertible to deposit rubles in another republic (since transactions must pass through correspondent accounts in central banks, which naturally place limits on the inter-republican credit they are prepared to extend). Several FSU republics have already introduced, or may soon introduce, their own currencies. The Russian authorities have announced their intention to establish full-fledged customs control at the Russian borders, and the Central Bank of Russia will soon introduce exchange rates between the Russian ruble and the rubles or other currencies of other FSU republics. Thus the creation of a common monetary area is no longer realistic.

> **Box 4.1**
> **Reasons for Export Licensing?**
>
> In early 1992, when Russia liberalized prices and Georgia still maintained price controls, export restrictions were necessary to prevent the outflow of goods from Georgia to Russia. However, with the liberalization of most prices in Georgia, this rationale for maintaining export licensing no longer obtains. The other reason given for requiring licensing is that Georgia has monopoly power in certain commodity markets, which it can exploit by maintaining restrictions on exports. However, this argument is also dubious. Except in the case of planes, Georgia is unlikely to have monopoly power for its products, even within the countries of the FSU (Table 3.5, Statistical Appendix). Georgia's share in total inter-regional trade may be large for some specific commodities such as tea, wine, tobacco, sub-tropical plants and specific fruits. But even in these cases, as soon as the purchasing power parity and the exchange rate are properly aligned, countries outside the region may emerge as competitors. For example, in the tea market, Georgia may have to compete with India, Kenya and Sri Lanka. In any case, it is obvious that the monopoly power argument can apply to only a very small fraction of Georgian exports; it does not provide a justification for the extensive licensing system that presently exists.
>
> For exports to FSU countries (but not to third countries) there could be a third reason for licensing. If Georgia wants to introduce its own currency, it may not want to continue to run trade surpluses and accumulate rubles (especially since after June 1992 Georgia could not buy dollars for rubles from the Russian market). For once a new currency is introduced, and rubles withdrawn from circulation, they are worthless: the government cannot take these rubles to Russia and claim goods in return. By restricting the issuing of licenses the government could control the trade balance, and the net inflow of rubles.*/ Of course, restrictions by one country on exports to another invites retaliation, with the result that overall trade contracts.
>
> ---
>
> */ For the same reason, countries may adopt a free import regime: buying goods from FSU countries for rubles would help get rid of ruble balances. As long as Georgia could buy dollars with rubles from the Russian market, imports from the rest of the world could also be effectively bought for rubles.

Georgia has responded to the difficulties in conducting inter-republican trade by negotiating trade treaties with other governments. Currently, it has binding trade treaties with nine republics and negotiations are underway with the remaining five, including Russia. In order to allow trade to reflect market forces and comparative advantage, it is important that government intervention in such trade be kept to a minimum and that, to the extent possible, enterprises be free to negotiate their best terms on price, credit and other aspects of the contract.[10] Barter, although it can be carried out on an enterprise to enterprise basis, is far less efficient and difficult to arrange than sales and purchases using money as a medium of exchange.

New payments arrangements will have to be developed if inter-republican trade is to contribute effectively to the restoration of output and growth in Georgia and other republics of the FSU. The sharp declines in intra-FSU trade have been a major contributory factor in the collapse of output, as enterprises lost both their sources of supply and their markets. While Georgia will no doubt intensify its trading relations with non-FSU trading partners, intra-FSU trade will remain dominant in the near term. Transitional payments arrangements need to be devised to facilitate this trade until the countries have established convertible currencies, reasonably stable exchange rates, and adequate international reserves.

A multilateral clearing union, which could cover all FSU republics, is an attractive and feasible approach. Even if the FSU participants are establishing current account convertibility with the rest of the world, as long as they have both a shortage of hard currency and trade intensively among themselves, multilateral clearing arrangements are desirable. They would greatly reduce the level of international reserves necessary to maintain relatively open trade policies. Such a multilateral clearing union would provide short-term credit and have relatively short settlement periods; at the end of each period each participant's net balance would be settled in convertible currency. Since there would be simultaneous settlement of all claims between participating central banks, the present tendency to seek bilateral balances would be eliminated. Enterprise to enterprise trade would be greatly facilitated.

Proposals have also been made for the establishment of a payments union, perhaps modeled on the European Payments Union of the 1950s. Such an arrangement would differ from a clearing union primarily in providing longer term credit to deficit members. Presently, FSU suppliers are unable to compete with those in other countries because the former lack the support of official export credit agencies. It is argued that the availability of credit would be a desirable incentive to encourage intra-FSU trade during a period when there are strong pressures in individual republics toward self-sufficiency and economic autarky. Providing relatively long-term credit to deficit republics, however, raises several difficult problems. Even if the likely surplus country, Russia, were willing to extend some credit to deficit members, and if substantial additional credit resources were provided by Western countries, there would have to be strict quotas beyond which deficits would be settled in convertible currencies. Participants with structural balance of payments deficits would be likely to soon exhaust their quotas, thus reducing the payments union to the equivalent of a clearing union. In addition, donors will normally insist that anything other than short-term balance of payments financing be accompanied by appropriate policy conditionality and monitoring. While creating a new FSU-area institution for this purpose thus raises many problems, a clearing union does seem feasible and would provide most of the advantages and none of the disadvantages of a payments union.

Endnotes

1.   Between December 1991 and July 1992, the import price of natural gas rose from Rbl 51 per thousand cubic meters to Rbl 1710; that of crude oil rose from Rbl 90 to Rbl 1000 per ton; and that of imported electricity from 5 kopeks to Rbl 1.93 per kwh (in the case of purchases from Russia) and to Rbl 4.72 per kwh (for purchases from Turkmenistan). For some of these products, the price set by the government reflects a mark up over the cost of imports, for example for coal and industrial fuel (imported from Russia) and natural gas (imported from Turkmenistan).

2.   Energy subsidies amounted to 11.8 percent of total state budget expenditures in 1992. However, price controls do not necessarily result in budgetary costs. For example, in the case of natural gas and electricity, consumer prices for households are maintained below the cost of imports, and the difference is made up by charging higher prices from industrial consumers. There is no cost to the budget. This is different from household heating where the difference between the cost of production and the consumer price is paid by the budget (to the Ministry of Architecture and Construction).

3.   These problems can be illustrated with the case of tobacco. The industry has been liberalized, but the factories have not raised prices, because profits so obtained would accrue to the state and not to the managers. Instead, the factories continue to sell cigarettes at Rbl 3 per pack to middlemen, who sell these in the market at Rbl 7 per pack. The profit they make in this way is shared with the managers of the factories. Indeed, the factories are now claiming a Rbl 30 million subsidy from the government because they are not profitable at Rbl 3 per pack!

4.   The policy has since been shelved.

5.   In January and February 1992 sugar was available in state stores for Rbl 24/kg, but then disappeared from stores. Central Soyuz, a cooperative long active in distribution of foodstuffs, initiated a four-month program (May-August) for supplying sugar at the price of Rbl 55/kg, with a ration of 1.5 kg per person per month. Before its introduction in May, the bazaar price for sugar was Rbl 120/kg while the state store price was Rbl 35/kg -- but sugar was not available in those stores. Since the Central Soyuz program was introduced, the bazaar price has fallen to Rbl 80/kg. Central Soyuz buys some of its sugar from domestic suppliers, but the bulk is imported. It receives no subsidies from the government, though Central Soyuz did receive preferential access to export licenses to facilitate the barter trade for sugar imports. Sugar prices were liberalized in July.

6.   The purchasing power parity (PPP) for a given commodity gives the exchange rate between, for example, the dollar and the ruble which will equalize the purchasing power of each currency in domestic and foreign markets. For instance, if one liter of milk is priced at Rbl 4 in Georgia and $1 in the US, the PPP for milk is Rbl 4 per dollar. If the exchange rate is also Rbl 4 per dollar, the purchasing power of each currency will be the same in Georgia and the US. The PPPs for a select group of commodities, based on their prices in Georgia and abroad in 1990 and early 1992, shows that in 1990 the PPPs ranged between Rbl 0.3 and 2.2 per dollar (Table 3.4, Statistical Appendix). The actual exchange rate of Rbl 0.58 per dollar until November 1990 and Rbl 1.7 per dollar for the remainder of 1990 were close to the PPPs. In 1992, however, in terms of PPP, the dollar is highly overvalued (and the ruble undervalued): the highest value of the PPP (among the commodities listed in Table 3.4, Statistical Appendix) is Rbl 20.5 per dollar, while the exchange rate through most of 1992 was well over Rbl 100 per dollar. A possible explanation for the divergence could be that the exchange rate is being determined essentially in the asset market: the lack of confidence in the ruble creates an excess demand for dollars leading to the depreciation of the ruble.

7.   On the one hand, the undervalued exchange rate itself provides a very strong incentive to export. However, this is negated by the pervasive quantitative export restrictions.

8.   In this sense, the initial conditions of the countries of the FSU are quite different from East and Central European countries undertaking economic reforms. In the latter, import restrictions in the form of tariffs and licensing were extensive and these barriers to competition were progressively eliminated. On the other hand, export licensing was maintained only for a limited number of commodities, many for purposes of maintaining inter-governmental protocols and for health and safety reasons.

9.   However, it is believed that in practice **all** goods, whether on the list or not and whether exported to the FSU countries or other countries, are subject to licensing.

10.   In this respect, the treaty with Ukraine which specifies quantities only, allows enterprises to negotiate prices, and does not balance trade bilaterally is superior to that with Turkmenistan which fixes quantities and prices and also balances trade bilaterally.

CHAPTER 5

Enterprise and Financial Sector Reform

It is by now well recognized that reforms that expose the economy to competition and market forces are very important but are not enough to improve the efficiency in resource allocation. Liberalization does not, by itself, provide the structures that are part and parcel of the checks and balances inherent to a well-functioning market economy (e.g., atomistic markets, property rights, binding contracts, public regulations etc). Without these structures, incentives may operate in perverse ways -- to the detriment of efficiency. Examples include the emergence of unregulated monopolies in the early phases of reform (or parasites as mentioned earlier); financial scandals as individuals exploit weaknesses in the regulatory framework; "spontaneous" privatization and decapitalization of state enterprises as "founding ministries" lose control to workers and managers; and continued lending to unprofitable, highly indebted state enterprises.

The most fundamental issue to be resolved is the question of property rights. While it is probably possible to run a clear cut state enterprise or a private firm efficiently, it is not possible to get anything like efficiency from an enterprise whose current and future ownership status are in limbo. Thus it is important, first, to identify as quickly as possible those activities and enterprises that are to be privatized, and those that will remain under state ownership even in the long term. Second, it is important to identify the "real" owner right away, and eliminate any ambiguity about who the owner is. Without clearly defined ownership rights, and legally recognized owners with an interest in the long term preservation and appreciation of the enterprises' capital, there is no discipline on enterprise managers, and little incentive for them to resist pressures to increase wages, or to improve their productivity. Privatization of state enterprises, whereby ownership of assets is transferred to clearly identified owners, is therefore of critical importance. How to accelerate privatization while maintaining transparency of the process becomes an immediate policy issue.

However, as experience in Poland, Hungary and Czechoslovakia has shown, even the best of privatization takes time, and there are certain activities that are unlikely to be privatized even in the long term (for example, public utilities). For these activities, alternative governance structures must be created that work within the existing state ownership but make management and workers sensitive to long-term profitability considerations. One solution which is being increasingly adopted in other countries is commercialization of enterprises, making management responsible to a Board of Directors. For this to work, however, there ought to be significant incentive for managers and directors to manage the enterprise well.

Enterprises will also not respond to market pressures if they continue to have access to state subsidies. Poor performance will simply result in increased transfers either directly from the budget or indirectly through the financial system, and there will be no incentive to restructure. Without a credible threat of closure, incentives to improve performance and become competitive get blunted. Hardening the budget constraint of enterprises, by eliminating (direct and indirect) subsidies to loss making activities, and creating a framework for restructuring and closure of these activities is therefore crucial.

I. THE ENTERPRISE SECTOR

Privatization

Georgia has already adopted a body of legislation and decrees governing the enterprise sector and privatization.[1] However, the legal framework is far from complete. One major missing law, which is still being debated in Parliament, concerns the division of state property and the question of ownership. What is also lacking is a well-publicized government strategy to give priority to these reforms in its legislative program. Such a strategy will provide some assurance to prospective participants in the privatization process, particularly foreign investors, that the necessary legal infrastructure will be created at least in parallel with the implementation of privatization.

The successful implementation of a privatization program requires detailed binding rules to ensure consistency and fairness. Some of the key issues that need to be addressed are listed in Box 5.1.

Box 5.1
THE LEGAL FRAMEWORK FOR PRIVATIZATION

In the absence of legislation which in other countries would be found in the general body of commercial laws, it is necessary that the privatization program include some of the key aspects. In addition, the unfamiliarity of most officials and enterprise managers with the mechanics of privatization means that laws and regulations must set out in an unambiguous and detailed way the functions to be undertaken by the participants in the process so as to minimize administrative discretion and ensure transparency and consistency. Work is underway in preparing implementing laws and regulations, which should at least cover the following issues:

Small scale:

(a)   the rights of workers to buy the enterprise at a discount.
(b)   the preparation of information on assets and liabilities and the right of the prospective buyers to inspect the premises and books of account before the auction.
(c)   the procedure for the conduct of the auction and the transfer of the business to the winning bidder.
(d)   the leasing procedure for the premises occupied by the business (the bidders will offer an annual rental and the highest bidder will take over the net assets at book value);

Medium and Large Scale (case by case):

(a)   the preparation by enterprises of privatization plans.
(b)   the criteria to be applied by the State Property Management Committee in reviewing privatization plans.
(c)   management buy-outs; and
(d)   the need for the break-up of monopolies.

Significant progress has been achieved in some aspects of privatization. Most of urban housing has been privatized (Box 5.2); and more than 50 percent of agricultural land has been transferred to the private sector (Box 5.3). While privatization of enterprises has been initiated only recently, "informal" privatization (through long term leases to the workers at low rents with an option to buy at low prices) has been occurring at a rapid pace. The State Property Management Committee (SPM) has recently put a stop to the automatic granting of such leases.

In mid-August 1992 the Government adopted the first State Program of Privatization of State and Municipality Owned Enterprises for 1992-93. It describes the principles to be followed in privatization, lists sectors that will not be privatized in the short term, and outlines how enterprises will be sold and what the institutional arrangements will be. Except for water and forestry resources, certain public utilities (such as large power plants, pipelines, the metro, etc.), hospitals, educational institutions, and institutions of historical importance, virtually everything else can be privatized in the medium term.

Strategy of Privatization. About 1400 enterprises/assets including large, medium and small scale enterprises were identified for privatization by SPM and local authorities. The government has already approved the first list of 752 enterprises and assets for sale by mid-1993, and the names of some 200 of these enterprises and assets have been published. Enterprises and assets to be privatized in the next few years include small scale, medium and large enterprises. Rightly, the government intends to adopt a flexible and pragmatic strategy for privatization. Different approaches to privatizing small, medium and large enterprises may be adopted depending on what is likely to work, including mass privatization schemes and the use of vouchers. Very important, the strategy allows a top-down and a bottom-up approach: privatization of enterprises could be initiated from the top by the SPM, ministries, or departments: or they can be initiated from the bottom by workers, managers and/or other potential investors including foreign investors. The emphasis on the bottom-up approach is especially appropriate; otherwise the limited implementation capacity of the official agencies could undermine the speed of privatization. The main elements of the privatization strategy are to:

(a)   give priority to the privatization of small-scale enterprises, particularly those which can influence the emergence and operation of a market infrastructure in the Georgian economy; and those inefficient enterprises that could impede the development of the economy and the emergence of a market. These enterprises include, inter-alia, retail and wholesale enterprises, consumer services, marketing and industrial goods, food and light industries, construction, and enterprises producing construction materials, etc.

(b)   commercialize the largest enterprises (the number and criteria are not yet defined) followed by individual or mass privatization. This involves: (i) corporatization of enterprises and transformation of the majority of enterprises into joint stock companies; (ii) privatization of selected large individual enterprises through the sale of shares to strategic future partners, without including vouchers; and (iii) privatization of selected large and medium enterprises through the use of financial intermediaries and voucher schemes.

(c)   encourage and build on enterprise and investor-initiated privatizations.

Basically, the strategy is a sound one. As experience with privatization in Eastern and Central Europe has shown, it is appropriate to emphasize simple, pragmatic and flexible approaches, rather than attempt sophisticated first best solutions which are a source of great delay (eg., privatization in Poland). Speed is essential to prevent asset stripping and other irresponsible practices. With changes in ownership announced but not implemented, managers and workers alike have every incentive to decapitalize the enterprise, increase wages and accumulate debts. Many countries are therefore putting increasing emphasis on finding simple solutions that can be implemented speedily, even if these may not always be first best. This is also the approach of the government.

The decentralization of privatization implied by the bottom-up approach is also desirable and reflects the experience in other countries. In order to accelerate privatization, and not make speed hostage to the nascent government institutions that are responsible for managing privatization, it is important that enterprises, or potential investors, be able to initiate privatization, prepare privatization plans and complete the transactions. However, it is equally important that there be transparent rules and regulations governing this process. With limited supervisory/regulatory control, there is danger that accelerated privatization schemes result in abuse and asset stripping, which could create a backlash against privatization (as happened in Hungary and Poland in the early stages of spontaneous privatization).

However rapid the government's privatization program may be, there are real, practical limits to the extent to which the process of privatization can be speeded up. There are simply too few people within and outside government who know how to develop privatization plans, evaluate different bids, negotiate transactions etc. The considerable uncertainty about the economic prospects and the macroeconomic situation is also likely to reduce the speed of privatization. If privatization will take time, it is important to provide appropriate structures in state owned enterprises which permit efficient operations. The emphasis in the government's strategy on commercializing state enterprises and making them responsible to a board of directors is the correct one in these circumstances. Quick commercialization will also prevent the asset stripping behavior mentioned in the paragraph above. Here again, though, the lack of qualified personnel could be the bottleneck.

While the government's privatization strategy recognizes the importance of corporatization, the process of corporatization is not well defined in the decree concerning the transformation of enterprises into joint stock companies. The decree does not indicate clearly which companies will be transformed and the criteria of transformation. A more comprehensive decree that addresses these issues is being prepared. In order to accelerate the process, it is desirable that the government adopt a decree on the immediate transformation into joint stock companies of all enterprises employing, for example, more than 150 or 200 people. A few natural monopolies or otherwise "strategic" enterprises could be excluded from corporatization as they will continue to form part of the core state sector. This mass corporatization approach would define property rights clearly and thus facilitate privatization.

Small Privatization. Recent experience has shown that small scale privatization can be accomplished relatively quickly, and success in this endeavor can relieve critical bottlenecks in both retail and wholesale distribution of goods.[2] Retail stores, transportation (trucking), warehouses etc. should be privatized rapidly.

Progress in small scale privatization has been slow. The only real progress has been in the city of Tbilisi, but even here the program is behind schedule -- auctions that were scheduled for November-December 1992 were held in March 1993. A list of objects to be privatized was prepared, including 600 small shops, 32 petrol stations, 14 unfinished buildings and a large number of cars and trucks. The March auctions covered only about 100 cars and trucks. As a next step, the city will privatize enterprises with less than 5 employees and covering less than 30 square meters of space. Two methods of sale are likely to be considered -- (i) competitive bidding and (ii) auctions. Anyone, including foreigners, can participate in the sales. Limited preferences may be given during privatization to employees in small enterprises (1-3 persons). Some conditions may also be imposed on the sale of food stores, e.g., the buyer must maintain the profile of the store for at least 3 years. These conditions are likely to inhibit the privatization process and should be avoided as far as possible. Since there is a risk that some of the assets will be stripped, specifically in the case of the unfinished buildings, it is desirable that the government accelerate the process of preparing the regulations and start the auctions as early as possible.

The government is still in the process of finalizing the law concerning the division of state owned property and has not yet decided which small enterprises belong to municipalities or autonomous republics and which are the property of the federal government. Experience in privatization in the East European countries has shown that the distribution of state property between the federal government and the municipalities can become contentious and there is a real risk that such disputes will delay privatization. One way to speed things up is for the government to begin selling small enterprises under federal law, but to reserve a share of proceeds to compensate the municipalities for their share of ownership.

It seems unlikely that the privatization of small enterprises and shops will extend to the land on which the enterprise is situated. Leases of 10 to 15 years are more likely. This restriction will reduce the attractiveness of the sale and delay the process (as in Hungary).[3]

Large Privatization. The plan is to complete the bulk of the sales of the 1100 large enterprises in 4 to 5 years.[4] This timetable is extremely ambitious: experience in other countries has shown large privatization to be a difficult and time consuming process; and where successful it has generally involved foreign participation.

The SPM has a sensible, pragmatic approach which combines top-down and bottom-up sales. In the top-down sales, a special commission with representatives of the SPM, the National Bank, the Ministry of Finance, and the enterprise analyze the firm's situation and decide if, when and how it will be sold.[5] Bottom-up sales can occur whenever an enterprise or a buyer (including foreign investor) submits a proposal that is judged by the line Ministry, SPM and the Council of Ministers as having merit. To be successful, it is important that there be clear and transparent criteria for evaluating different proposals, and that the SPM have the technical capacity and the authority to decide quickly on the merits of the proposals. Otherwise, as was the experience in other countries, there is the danger that investor-led privatization schemes would be stifled. The expectation is that most large enterprises will either be transformed into joint stock companies and their shares sold or distributed free, or they will be sold through trade sales with competitive bidding.

Mass Privatization. Mass privatization is intended to speed up the pace of privatization of medium and large sized enterprises, build political support for privatization, and improve equity through the widespread distribution of shares to the population. In the privatization program for 1992-1993, the government stated its intention to make use of a certificate or voucher scheme. The SPM is designing a voucher program which is based on the model adopted in Russia. Under this plan, there will be a series of tranches, the first of which will be introduced in 1993. Vouchers will be issued to all Georgian citizens, including children, non-Georgian residents, and citizens living abroad. They will be freely tradeable. Unlike the Russian model, however, the present plan does not envisage printing a nominal value on the voucher. The SPM is also working, together with ministries, in identifying medium and large enterprises that will be privatized through vouchers.

However, significant policy decisions are still pending with regard to the voucher scheme. Given the limited time frame, detailed design and implementation planning are required. It is important that the objective of achieving widespread public shareholding be balanced with the need to provide effective ownership control. An effective program to support voucher distribution, usage and free market trade will need to consider the following elements:

(a)   give priority to administrative simplicity; other goals such as equity and revenue maximization are important but secondary. The scheme should avoid mechanisms that require detailed valuation or complex share distribution to the public: thus, it may be desirable to distribute the vouchers free to the public;

(b)   speed of distribution is critical. It is also important to implement the program in sequential tranches of firms to enable testing of design and adjustment of program in the light of experience;

(c)   privatization should be designed to allow sales to controlling shareholders who will pressure management for better performance. The percentage of shares to be distributed through the voucher system should not exceed 30 percent of total assets and the shares to go to the employees should not exceed 20 percent. Widely disbursed ownership through non-trading vouchers, employees shares or sales to small shareholders will not provide the "living, breathing entrepreneur" so important for management turnarounds.

(d)   vouchers should be tradable. An important advantage of being able to trade vouchers (for cash) is that it provides a means by which the number of voucher holders can be consolidated, enabling concentration of ownership that is necessary for effective governance. Putting a face value on the vouchers may also be advantageous as it eases trading. To maintain the value of the vouchers it is important that they be allowed to purchase a wide variety of assets such as land, unfinished construction sites, and small shops, in addition to the large state enterprises. Moreover, in order to reduce the inflationary impact of tradable vouchers, these should be issued in tranches that are tradable for a limited period only.

Investment Funds. Careful analysis should be undertaken with regard to the distribution of vouchers directly to the population or via financial intermediaries. The latter may be useful in concentrating ownership. However, a pre-requisite is a Capital Market Law which would regulate, among other things, the functioning of the investment funds and the stock exchange. In addition, if shares are to be placed with financial intermediaries, the following considerations should be kept in mind:

-    the selection of companies for mass privatization should be done by the SPM and not the financial intermediary.

-    to prevent monopolies, investment funds should not be sector specific.

-    one of the financial intermediaries (investment company) should be encouraged to play the role of active shareholder which will restructure, manage and sell the company.

Other passive intermediaries that could be considered include banks, pension funds and mutual funds.

- the remuneration for managers/agents of the investment funds should be success-based.

There remain considerable differences in government regarding the appropriate distribution of enterprise shares. Under the current law, 20 percent of enterprise shares are to be given free to the workers, with an additional 10 percent available to them at a discount. The remaining 70 percent of shares are to be sold for cash or vouchers. However, enterprise directors are demanding that they have the right to purchase controlling interest (51 percent) in their enterprise.

Some preference to workers and managers in the privatization of their enterprises makes sense insofar as it overcomes their fear of loss of employment or control of the enterprise and thus reduces their resistance to privatization. However, these preferences must be so designed that they do not inhibit outside strategic investors from obtaining controlling interest, thus discouraging new capital investment. Moreover, in view of the difficulties in assessing the value of enterprise assets, and hence the actual discount, it is better to simply give additional free shares to the employees.

Some Other Issues In Privatization

Privatization and Demonopolization. As in the other republics of the FSU, the productive sector, especially industry but also domestic trade, are highly concentrated and market competition is non-existent (<u>Annex 1</u>). In this situation, privatization would merely transform a state monopoly into a private monopoly, which would not necessarily improve efficiency. The solution is to create competition by facilitating entry of new enterprises, or through imports. To the extent existing state monopolies could be readily broken up (for example, in wholesale or retail trade; construction enterprises; wine-making enterprises; in manufacturing where production is undertaken in multiple plants), it is desirable that this be done prior to privatization. Effective anti-monopoly legislation should be enacted and an anti-Monopoly Committee established to monitor and enforce compliance with the law. Privatization and corporatization proposals for selected large, vertically integrated monopolies should be screened by the anti-monopoly committee.

Regulatory Framework. An appropriate regulatory framework must be put in place prior to or simultaneously with privatization. In the tradeable, commercially-oriented sector, regulatory provisions entailing removal of barriers (if any) to competition will have to be introduced. In the non-tradable utilities sectors which generally require large investments (such as electric power, water supply), establishment of independent regulatory bodies would be essential to assure private investors' confidence and long term economic and financial efficiency.

Bank Lending for Privatization. Currently, banks are free to lend for the purchase of enterprises. Such loans will need to be carefully regulated. Some so-called private banks are being created with the capital of public enterprises, and there is a risk that these enterprises use their own capital to purchase themselves. And where the banking system is public or quasi-public (i.e., banks owned by ministry or state enterprise employees), leverage or the sale by bank debt does little to sever the ties with the state. It would be better to give buyers 4 to 5 years to pay for the enterprise and prepare for the possibility of default by developing penalties for non-payment and plans on how to treat defaults. Experience elsewhere also shows that if banks are allowed to accept the shares that the buyer intends to purchase as collateral, a speculative bubble can be created: the credit increases the value of the shares, which can then be used for more borrowing and which further increases share value, and so forth. When the collapse of the share value occurs, which is highly probable, the entire banking system may be put at risk.

Use of Privatization Proceeds. While there is as yet no explicit policy on how to use the revenues that may be generated through privatization, various ideas are being considered. These include social safety net projects, assistance for development of entrepreneurship and small enterprises and the financing of part of the budget deficit. Since these privatization proceeds are one time windfalls, they should not be treated like regular revenues. In particular it could be unwise to use these funds to begin on-going programs (such as social safety net) that will require recurrent expenditures later, unless some other future funding source is assured.

Private Sector Development

New private ventures are expected to provide the impetus to growth in the medium term. They will also be the source of competition to the existing state enterprises. Though Georgia has a tradition of unrecorded private sector economic activity, this needs to be fostered and integrated into the economic mainstream. Private sector development will be promoted by most of the measures already outlined, including the liberalization of prices and imports, the elimination of budgetary support to the state sector, privatization, etc.. The development of an efficient financial sector (see below) is also important. In addition, the following measures are essential.

First, an appropriate legal framework for private sector activity must be developed, including for example, the mining code, mortgage laws etc.. In addition, institutions such as the arbitrage and judicial system to enable resolution of commercial conflicts need to be established. Second, it is important to identify unnecessary regulations that block private sector activity or increase the cost of entry. Such deficiencies in current regulations must be eliminated. Adoption of simple, automatic licensing or registration procedures to facilitate entry should be accorded priority. Third, it is necessary to improve the system of taxation. Reforms should aim at broadening the tax base and at simplifying tax administration (for example, the VAT).

The lack of availability of office space, land or workshops are often important constraints to the growth of the private sector. Municipalities should be encouraged to identify property that has potential for commercial use and make it available for lease or for privatization. And finally, the government should mobilize external assistance (preferably grants) to finance entrepreneurial development and training, including dissemination of information, promotion of contacts with foreign markets, assistance in setting up business advisory services etc. (see Annex 1).

Box 5.2
PRIVATIZATION OF HOUSING

Georgia is out in front of other republics of the FSU in privatizing urban housing. Some 28 percent of housing has been privatized since the program began in March 1992, and the expectation is that all houses will be private by the end of the year. Every day some 300 apartments are transferred, free of charge, to the tenants. Transfer of housing is free to the present tenants, who have only to pay the costs of the transfer and titling (Rbl 400- 600) and the equivalent of a two year lease as an advance to ensure that funds are available for major restorations or innovations. These privatizations are carried out by the Office of Communal Services and are under the supervision of the SPM and its branches.

Once the titles are given, the new owner is free to sell or otherwise transfer the housing. There is some possibility of restitution of land to former owners, especially to victims of the 1937 nationalizations; this is being considered on a case by case basis and has not happened yet. A final decision on the treatment of restitution will be made after the elections.

Georgia already has long experience with private housing. 95 percent of rural housing was and is private and close to half the population is rural. This may make it easier to establish a fully operating housing market. Right now, however, the market is thin and the prices high (a one bedroom apartment with 25 square meters of usable space costs Rbl 150,000 in a less desirable suburb of Tbilisi, about Rbl 1 million in a good district, compared to an average annual wage income in mid-1992 of Rbl 7500.

The government plans to help reduce the housing shortage by building free homes for all those on the waiting list for housing (about 100,000). The costs of construction has risen sharply with the freeing of prices and there is little private construction going on. The government hopes to finance the new construction with a property tax (none exists yet) and the savings from maintenance charges which used to be paid by the state. By introducing a property tax as soon as possible the government will not only raise funds it can use for housing construction, it will also encourage people who have more space than they need to sell, bringing down the price of housing and helping ease the shortage. New housing construction can be done through competitive bidding open to private construction companies as a way to encourage the emergence of new private firms (some observers claim that over 40 percent of construction enterprises are now private).

While the free transfer of housing helps speed privatization and the emergence of a housing market, it raises some concerns that need to be addressed. First, since rents in the past did not cover the costs of maintenance, the new owners are facing the real cost of maintenance for the first time. There is a risk that people will be less willing to spend to maintain an asset they received for free since there is no way for them to weigh the cost against the value of a free good. The rapid emergence of an active housing market is crucial if people are to understand the value of housing and maintenance.

Even more important, people may not spend to maintain common areas in large apartment buildings unless there is some mechanism to prevent free riders -- people who benefit from the efforts of others to maintain the building. These institutions may emerge spontaneously. Although the municipalities had responsibility for maintenance in the past, they often failed to maintain the buildings and the tenants had to chip in to, for example, repair the elevators or even the electrical substation. The government could make it easier for the new apartment owners to organize by producing model condominium and cooperative agreements which the municipalities could distribute to help tenants form associations. The contracts for condominiums and cooperatives are not complex and many models exist which could be adapted to the needs of Georgia and its different municipalities.

The broader legal and institutional framework for a private housing market is complex, involving such issues as the development of a mortgage finance system, with liens, foreclosure and eviction procedures, as well as zoning regulations, construction standards, tenants rights, rules on inheritance and transfer. Since housing is rapidly becoming private, it will be crucial to put the minimum legal framework in place for the emergence of a housing market. An active market in housing is the fastest way to begin to ease the housing shortage and to ensure that the new owners understand that property, even free property, entails costs and responsibilities that they, not the state, must meet.

Box 5.3
PRIVATIZATION OF LAND

Georgia has also made rapid strides in privatizing agricultural land. There are 1,150,000 hectares of cultivated lands in Georgia. Until 1991, only 6 percent of this land was privately owned. By the spring of 1992, 50 percent were distributed free of charge to citizens and farmers according to well-defined policy. By the end of 1993, the government intends to privatize 70-75 percent of the land. The remaining 20-25 percent will remain the property of the State and will be mainly used for production of seeds.

The land is distributed by a village commission which is elected in a village meeting and has full authority to decide who is eligible for which land. All village residents (and urban dwellers with family in the village) have a right to apply. The land can be traded two years after title is received. Titling seems to be proceeding reasonably rapidly: titles had been distributed for 300,000 of the 400,000 hectares distributed.

The farmland remaining in state hands is in large plantations of 500 to 1000 hectares, mostly state farms associated with agro-industry and agricultural research. The legislation concerning these lands is not yet decided. The government thinks it would be uneconomic to break these farms up, and since few in Georgia could purchase them outright, it is likely they will be transformed into joint stock companies and the shares will be sold. Interested foreign investors can also form joint ventures with these farms.

The Ministry of Agriculture is not expecting the reform to reduce agricultural production. Georgians have a long tradition of growing abundant supplies on their own plots, which, as in other parts of the FSU, were significantly more productive than the state lands (see Table 6.2-6.3, Statistical Appendix). If that pattern continues to hold, the redistribution of land may actually increase total production. The main constraint will be the increasing cost of production and the unavailability of credit as the stabilization program is implemented.

Also, as the government is the first to admit, the farms are too small. The Ministry of Agriculture estimates that 5 hectares of good land is the minimum to support a farming family. And the machinery is large and uneconomic for these small farms. Georgia does not have the foreign exchange to import smaller farm machinery, or the raw materials to manufacture it. Fortunately, the state farms had a lot of excess equipment and cooperatives have already been created to sell machinery services to farmers. This may ease the situation somewhat, but as these farms switch to the more intensive agriculture suited for small plots they will need smaller scale equipment.

One simple and rapid way to reduce the risk of a production fall is to allow farmers to sell their property as soon as they receive title. That way land can be consolidated into viable farms and those with interest in and knowledge of farming can purchase land from those who are not interested in agriculture. The argument given against this (that naive new owners will sell too soon and too low) is one of outmoded paternalism. A few may be naive, but most new owners will quickly learn the value of their asset. If government is worried about the workings of a new land market, it can help by financing a private information service to track land prices and supply them to local newspapers. A land tax may also discourage speculators from buying land to hold it idle. Such a tax could vary by land use: higher taxes on land held idle or used for non-agricultural purposes, lower taxes on land shown to be used for agriculture. Another argument is that it might appear inequitable if those who received land for free quickly exchanged it for cash. The appearance of inequity is always politically sensitive, but it will also be highly inequitable if the free distribution of land is seen to result in a drop in production and an increase in food prices for the urban population.

State Ownership and Improved Corporate Governance

Even under the best of conditions, a large number of enterprises will remain state owned for a long time. This is because of several factors, including: (i) the sheer size of the state enterprise sector; (ii) the uncertain demand for many state enterprises that are to be privatized; and (iii) the complex nature of many privatization transactions, especially when the infrastructure for facilitating these transactions and persons experienced in dealing with them are lacking. Therefore, even as efforts are made to accelerate privatization, it is necessary to address directly the problem of those enterprises that are likely to remain under state ownership. The aim must be to facilitate effective exercise of government ownership through appropriate institutions, in such a way as not to slow down the privatization process.

Corporatization. As in other parts of the FSU, one of the main problems in these enterprises is that though they are state owned, a "real" owner, capable of ensuring the preservation and appreciation of the value of enterprise assets, does not exist. Typically, state enterprises are under the supervision of the branch ministries and their structure does not appropriately distinguish the rights and responsibilities of owners and managers. Thus for example, even though the ownership of industrial enterprises targeted for privatization was recently transferred to the SPM from the branch ministries, the management of these enterprises is still overseen by the branch ministries, who are also responsible for the appointment of managers. One solution, which is reflected in the government's privatization strategy (see para. 9) is to quickly corporatize (transform into joint stock companies) all state enterprises over a certain size. This transformation will confirm the state's ownership rights on these enterprises, and make their structure conform to modern company forms. This in turn will encourage subsequent privatization and the participation of foreign investors. In the new company form, the government as owner would: (i) select and appoint competent and qualified persons to enterprise boards through a public and transparent process; (ii) provide management with clear objectives; (iii) agree with management on enterprise strategy; (iv) leave management as free as needed to achieve the agreed objectives; and (v) oblige management to full and transparent accountability.

Currently, all state enterprises are either the responsibility of the branch ministry or the SMP (if the enterprise is targeted for privatization). After transformation, the branch ministry or the SPM would exercise the state's ownership rights through company boards, which would be responsible for strategic decisions and management oversight, and should also provide outside guidance to management. The SPM could also contract out management to private contractors. It is very clear that if the SPM is to perform its functions effectively, it will have to be strengthened considerably.

In this framework, effective management will depend very much on the quality and competence of the company boards. In order to strengthen these boards, it may be necessary to (i) establish clear criteria for the selection of board members; (ii) develop appropriate remuneration policy that will provide incentives to board members; and (iii) provide training to the members. Nevertheless, the shortage of qualified people will remain a constraint to effective governance in the short and medium term.

Hardening the Budget Constraint. Without financial discipline, which requires enterprise owners, managers and workers be held accountable for their decisions, incentives to increase efficiency are blunted. Sensitivity to price signals is less if profitability does not matter and losses are covered by either the government or the financial system. Thus strengthening financial discipline is essential to induce a positive supply response. At the macro level, this requires that credit policies are strict, and that bank loans are made available only to creditworthy enterprises, and at the right price. It also means that the government does not subsidize the operations of loss-making enterprises through subsidies or tax forgiveness or the build up of arrears. At the micro level, financial discipline requires that enterprises maintain payment discipline, and arrears, either to suppliers of inputs or to banks, are not tolerated. In the final analysis, financial discipline requires there be a credible threat of closure for unprofitable enterprises.

Unlike in market economies, the lack of domestic and foreign competition, and the absence of any framework for restructuring and liquidation, contributes to lax financial discipline. If there is only one domestic supplier, and imports are not a viable option, the supplier does not face a credible threat of closure. Similarly, if there are only a few large buyers, they have less to worry from sanctions against non-payment. Greater competition is essential. That is why greater import competition and entry of new firms are so important. In addition, unprofitable firms continue to be subsidized, directly or indirectly. For example, enterprises continue to receive loans from banks at negative real interest rates, which are in turn financed by subsidized refinancing loans from the NBG.[6] Direct budgetary subsidies to enterprises also exist, though their size is not known.

To tighten financial discipline, it is necessary that subsidies to loss-making activities be phased out. To the extent subsidies must be maintained to serve social needs, these should be explicitly budgeted rather than channeled through the financial system. This would not only make the cost of subsidization transparent; it would also avoid distorting the incentives to save and invest in profitable activities. Progressive reduction of the budgetary subsidies could be linked with the adoption of satisfactory restructuring plans.

Finally, it is necessary to send out a signal that unprofitable enterprises will not be bailed out indefinitely. For this it may be essential for the government to target a few unviable state enterprises for restructuring or closure.

As in many other countries of the FSU, and eastern and central Europe in the early stages of stabilization, there has been a large increase in arrears: enterprises simply do not pay each other, or banks, for receipt of goods and services. The stock of unpaid bills, which amounted to Rbl 3.2 billion at the end of 1991 increased to Rbl 20.6 billion by end-November 1992. Most of these were arrears on payment to Russian enterprises. These arrears mostly concern state-owned firms that have been forced to cut back production due to the disruption in trade with other republics.

There is no simple solution to the problem of arrears. To some extent, it is a manifestation of cash "shortage" discussed in chapter 1. The solution to that problem lies in encouraging financial intermediation which will provide banks the liquidity to pass on to its clients who are mainly state enterprises. Improvements in inter-regional payments mechanism is vital. Greater competition is also necessary to enforce payment discipline. This will be facilitated by increased imports and by encouraging the growth of new private ventures (see below). Finally, banks and other enterprises should be encouraged to initiate the restructuring of illiquid clients. And it may be desirable to maintain and publicize information about the most prominent defaulters so that potential creditors are well aware of the risks they are incurring.

II. THE FINANCIAL SECTOR

As discussed in Chapter 2, the medium term prospects for economic recovery depends very much on increasing the rate of savings in the economy, and utilizing the savings for efficient investments. An efficient financial system is necessary to do that. However, just as enterprise sector reform is necessary to generate an efficient supply response from enterprises, financial sector reforms are required to provide banks and other financial institutions the incentive to mobilize financial resources and to allocate these efficiently. As suggested in chapter 1, savings deposits in banks have shrunk considerably in recent months, suggesting a process of financial dis-intermediation. The ratio of the stock of saving and time deposits to GDP fell from 93 percent in end December 1991 to 58 percent by end December 1992. This trend will have to be reversed and confidence restored in the banking system. The allocation of credit is also distorted. An important reason for this is that banking activities continue to be directed by the state, either directly through government dictate, or indirectly by the refinancing policies of the NBG. This is not consistent with market based resource allocation, and will only contribute to inefficiencies. On the other hand, merely liberalizing the financial market will not do. For example, as long as banks continue to depend heavily on low cost resources of the NBG for making loans, there is little incentive for them to raise interest rates to mobilize deposits of the population. Similarly, if the state continues to bail out loss making activities higher interest rates will not select the more profitable investments: indeed the more viable investments may be crowded out by the least profitable ones. Appropriate prudential regulations and effective supervision capacities are needed to ensure banks behave responsibly.

The ownership structure of banks also exacerbates the problem: banks are largely owned by state enterprises who are also their clients. Indeed, many new banks have been created with the sole objective of raising funds for their owners. This situation is fraught with danger, as the experience in Yugoslavia has shown: banks will continue to lend to their owners irrespective of profitability, and scarce financial resources that would otherwise be available for efficient activities would be diverted to loss-making ones.

Ultimately, enterprise and financial sector reforms are closely linked. If enterprises begin to perform well, the health of the financial system will improve: after all enterprises are the main clients of banks. On the other hand, if loss-making enterprises are kept alive (either by budget subsidies, or bank loans) and enterprise reform delayed, this will adversely affect the financial system. To the extent the financial system subsidizes the loss-making activities, this is done either by taxing savings (by maintaining low interest rates on saving) or by taxing efficient activities (by maintaining high interest rates on lending). Either way, efficient financial intermediation will be a victim.

Description of the Financial System

As of mid-1992 the financial system comprises the National Bank of Georgia (NBG), 5 specialized state "commercial" banks, and 71 "private" commercial banks (see Box 5.4). Despite the large number of private banks, the five state banks account for roughly 85 percent of total credit. The specialized state banks are the Agroprombank, which lends primarily to the agricultural sector; the Promstoibank, which largely finances heavy industry and major construction activities; the Gilsotsbank, which concentrates on light industry and trade; the Vneshekonombank, which used to specialize in foreign exchange transactions; and the Sberbank, which is the main savings bank for the population. Of the 71 private banks, only one is wholly private and one has majority private ownership. The rest are owned largely by state enterprises.

Despite the separation of the National Bank from the commercial banks, the system effectively is a one-tier system. The NBG services the deposits of the Savings Bank and earns interest from refinancing credits to the specialized state banks. And most of the lending of the specialized banks in 1992 was based on refinancing credits from the NBG. Thus the NBG is the dominant factor in determining the interest rates on deposits of households, and it directs the allocation of credit in the economy. The main instruments of monetary control are the interest rates on household deposits with the Savings bank, and the interest rates and volume of refinance credits to the specialized state banks. Other interest rates are freely determined by banks.

Mobilization of Financial Savings

In contrast to 1991, when savings deposits of households increased by 34 percent, virtually no new deposits were recorded in the first half of 1992.[7] Enterprise deposits in the three specialized state banks also rose slowly: they grew by 36 percent in the first five months of 1992 when the retail price index rose more than 400 percent. In July, in order to partially compensate for inflation, deposits in the Savings Bank were doubled in value. This resulted in a temporary inflow of Rbl 5 billion of deposits. Nevertheless, the ratio of savings and time deposits to GDP fell from 93 percent in end December 1991 to 58 percent by end December 1992. Reversing these trends must be a major objective of financial sector reforms.

The drying up of household and enterprise deposits is due to several factors. First, the interest rate offered by the Savings Bank on household saving deposits and certificates of deposits is negative in real terms: 4.5 percent in nominal terms in 1991, rising to roughly 20 percent by end-1992. Interest rate on demand deposits of enterprises ranged between 30-35 percent. With an inflation rate of over 1000 percent in the last two years, the real returns on these savings are strongly negative. Second, the shortage of currency has resulted in limiting withdrawal rights on savings accounts. This disparity in liquidity of savings deposits and cash has led to the phenomenon of premia on cash rubles over "non-cash" rubles, and has contributed to the reluctance to place deposits in banks.

To mobilize savings, interest rates on deposits will have to rise. While banks (other than the Savings Bank) are free to set their own interest rates on deposits, the low interest rates on refinancing credits from the NBG provides them no incentive to do so.[8] To encourage banks to mobilize savings from households, the NBG should increase its refinance rate (currently only 40 percent) to a level higher than the maximum deposit rate in the market.

Almost all of household deposits are with the Savings Bank. Yet, as a result of the break-up of the FSU it has no offsetting assets. The NBG has taken over the responsibility of servicing the interest payments and the security of the deposit. Interest rates on these deposits are fixed by the NBG and are currently extremely low, ranging from 2 percent for sight deposits and 9 percent for long term deposits. Until such time as the Savings Bank is granted financial independence, the NBG should increase interest rates on household deposits with the Savings Bank.

Currently, reserve requirements are set by the NBG at 20 percent of total liabilities (including capital) by the NBG.[9] However, reserve requirements for specialized banks are not fully enforced. Since shortfalls in meeting these requirements are also a form of borrowing from the NBG, the NBG should ensure full compliance from all banks in meeting the requirements. If there are shortfalls, interest on these shortfalls should be set at penalty rates in excess of the refinance rate.

Increasing interest rates may not be enough to promote savings if confidence in the banking system is not restored. In this context, continued limits on withdrawal of savings deposits are counterproductive. As mentioned in Chapter 1, they will only accelerate financial disintermediation and not serve to mitigate the cash shortage they were meant to address.

```
Box 5.4
THE FINANCIAL SYSTEM IN GEORGIA*/
```

Since Georgia became independent, the financial system comprises the National Bank of Georgia, five specialized "state commercial banks", and private commercial banks. The banking system is highly concentrated and the five state banks control 85 percent of credit. Of the private commercial banks, there is only one wholly private bank, and one bank that has majority private ownership. The remainder of the new private banks are owned by state enterprises.

The activities of the financial system are regulated by three laws issued in August 1991: the law "On the National Bank of Georgia", the Law "On Monetary and Credit Regulations in Georgia, and the law "On Banks and Banking Activities in Georgia".

The National Bank of Georgia

As in most other economies, the NBG is responsible for maintaining the stability of the national currency in the context of sustainable economic growth. The NBG is independent of the government and is responsible only to the Supreme Council of the Republic. Except in special circumstances the law prohibits the NBG from financing deficits of the state budget.

The main functions of the NBG are: issuing of currency and organizing its circulation through the money market; setting the exchange rate; monetary and credit regulation; managing the national debt; managing international reserves; being a lender of last resort to the banks; organization of payments; regulating the security and foreign currency markets; supervision of commercial banks; and setting up a system for gathering information statistics on the banking system.

The law "On Monetary and Credit Regulations" lists the principal instruments which can be used by the National Bank to achieve its control of the money supply. These include (i) ceilings on expansion of credits extended by commercial banks; setting the volume and the price (interest rate) of refinancing credits extended to commercial banks; and fixing reserve requirements. Commercial banks are free to set their own deposit and lending interest rates.

The State Commercial Banks

The state commercial banks were previously domestic branches of the specialized financial institutions of the Soviet Union. They were nationalized in April 1991 and their assets and liabilities towards the center were taken over by the National Bank of Georgia. The state commercial banks include three banks that provide credits to different sectors, the Savings Bank (Sberbank Georgia) and the foreign trade bank (Eximbank, formerly Vneshekonombank Georgia).

(i) The Specialized Lending Banks

These three banks are: The Agricultural Bank (Agroprombank-Georgia); the Bank for Industry and Construction (Promstroibank-Georgia); the Social Development Bank (Gilsotsbank-Georgia). Their combined loan portfolio at the end of May 1992 amounted to Rbl 24 billion, an increase of 100 percent since end 1991 and representing 80 percent of total credit to the economy. The main items on the liability side are National Bank refinancing (Rbl 16.7 billion) and enterprises deposits (Rbl 5.6 billion). Most of the credit expansion over the first five months of 1992 relate to state-ordered loans and were financed by the increase in refinancing from the National Bank.

The Agricultural Bank is the largest bank in Georgia in terms of the size of its loan portfolio (Rbl 8-9 billion). Most of its loans are for food processing and raw material processing enterprises. The bank has 78 branches and employs 1500 people. Apparently, there was only a slight increase in its loan portfolio in the first half of 1992. The current interest rates on loans range between 40-60 percent.

The Bank for Industry and Construction. The bank has 26 regional branches and a staff of 1100. It finances heavy industry and major construction activities. It is also financing industries in serious financial difficulties. About 10-15 factories that are making losses and must be restructured are being financed by the bank at the behest of the state. The bank's loan portfolio amounts to Rbl 9 billion showing a very large increase compared to the Rbl 2 billion estimate in March 1992. As its own deposit resources are relatively low (Rbl 1.7 billion), it must have absorbed much of the increase in the National Bank refinancing over the last months. The bank intends to attract more deposits, particularly from households, by raising interest rates up to 25-40 percent depending on the term of deposits (up to 5 years). In order to collect enough cash resources for ensuring the liquidity of its deposits, the bank requires its loans be partly repaid in cash. The cash repayment can vary from 50-80 percent for easily tradable goods. Wages paid by the bank are regulated by the state. Current interest rates on loans range between 65-80 percent.

*/ As of mid-1992

Box 5.4 continued

The Bank of Social Development of Housing and Communal Economy has 43 branches and employs 1200 people. Lending operations are concentrated on light industry, and trading. The total loan portfolio is Rbl 6.5 billion of which Rbl 2 billion are long term loans. The bank is the main source of long term credit (74 percent of the total), mainly for buildings. With a relatively large deposit base (Rbl 4.5 billion), dependence on NBG refinancing is limited. Seventy percent of the stock of loans has been granted on government orders. The interest rate charged on credits issued with refinancing from NBG is 50-60 percent, while interest rates on loans based on own resources vary widely (and can be as low as 5 percent). On the liability side, time deposits from organizations are paid an interest between 15-20 percent according to the maturity and the amount of the deposit. Sight deposits are not renumerated. In comparison with other banks, the quality of the loans portfolio is said to be quite good and arrears under control. The bank intends to become a major competitor to the Savings Bank for collecting deposits from individuals.

(ii) The State Commercial Savings Bank

The Savings Bank has 86 branches and 1100 affiliated offices, some of them in post offices. It has a staff of 4600 and 3.2 million household depositors. Georgians used to be among the biggest savers in the former Soviet Union and Georgia ranked second (after Lithuania) in terms of deposits per capita. Currently, deposits amount to Rbl 13.4 billion. This includes Rbl 3 billion corresponding to the 40 percent "compensation" decided last year. At first these amounts were to be frozen for 3 years, but it was then decided to credit them to the depositors accounts in June 1992. However, this decision had little practical effect as, given the shortage of cash, the Savings Bank cannot comply with withdrawals requests. As a result of their near total illiquidity, deposits on savings accounts (aside from the compensation) stopped growing during the first part of 1992. The rates of interest paid on savings accounts are decided by the Government. In June 1992, these ranged from 2 percent for sight deposits to 9 percent for long term deposits. A new compensation scheme, at a rate of 100 percent, was introduced in July 1992. This led to a temporary inflow of deposits equivalent to Rbl 5 billion.

Before 1991, all deposits collected by the Savings Bank were centralized to Moscow which used the funds. The Bank did not have any significant credit activity of its own. After independence, the claim on Moscow is now held by the National Bank which is liable towards the Savings Bank for paying interest and guaranteeing the deposits. In 1991, the Bank was also ordered by the new government to grant loans amounting to Rbl 3.5 billion to some commercial organizations. Currently the interest rate on loans from the Savings Bank is about 100 percent.

(iii) The Foreign Trade Bank

The Eximbank is the official successor of the Georgian branch of the former Vneshekonombank-USSR which specialized in carrying out foreign exchange banking transactions and helping domestic producers engaged in international trade operations. The new Eximbank was granted a general license allowing it to open correspondent accounts abroad. The bank seems to play an important part in foreign trade operations but its total resources (a few hundred million rubles, mainly ruble deposits of enterprises engaged in international trade) is quite small in comparison to other state banks.

It is currently planned that in the near future all these state commercial banks will be privatized and turned into joint stock companies. Banks are enthusiastic about this prospect and believe they will be able to raise additional resources by issuing shares and make greater profits once they are independent. However, this widely share optimism does not seem to take into account the risks of banking operations in a market economy which will be particularly high in Georgia given the present situation of many borrowers.

Private Commercial Banks

Currently, there are 71 private commercial banks. At the end of May 1992, they accounted for about 20 percent of enterprise deposits and 12 percent of the short term credits to the economy. Over the first five months of the year, the increase in these credits amounted to more than 160 percent despite the fact that private banks have not had access to the refinancing of the National Bank during this period. Long term credit for investment purposes is still limited as there is no regulatory framework and no bankruptcy law. A significant part of the bank resources is constituted by paid-in capital so that the level of the capital to credit ratio can be considered reasonably high (30 percent in January 1992, 20 percent in June).

The interest rate policies have been more audacious than in the state banks, reflecting competition for attracting deposits: typical annual rates are 25 percent for sight deposits, 40 percent for 1 to 3 years term deposits and up to 100 percent for 10 years deposits. Rates charged to borrowers vary from an annual 70 percent to a monthly 10 percent. Better conditions can be granted when the loan is repaid in cash.

Allocation of Credit

Directed Credits. The allocation of credit is largely determined by the state through refinancing from the NBG.[10] Almost 88 percent of the total credit expansion in the first half of 1992 came from the three specialized banks, and the bulk of their credit expansion was based on refinancing from the NBG. These credits were extended by the NBG to finance agreed upon and critical projects, which were chosen by the NBG based on recommendations by the Ministries.[11] Interest rates charged on loans by commercial banks were around 60-90 percent.[12]

Directed credits from the NBG are not consistent with a decentralized, market based financial system. This practice will not encourage credit to flow to the most efficient users and the private sector will continue to be crowded out. In the short term, the use of directed credits should be strictly limited to a few activities. Over time they should be phased out and banks should be encouraged to obtain their resources from the inter-bank market rather than the NBG (for example by progressively increasing the cost of these credits for different tranches). Access to refinancing credits should be based on clear rules, linked for example to the capital of the bank. It should not distinguish between particular activities.

Non-Performing Loans. Non-performing loans are another reason for distorting the allocation of new credit as loans are likely to flow to uncreditworthy borrowers to pay wages or service old debts. Most of the specialized state banks have unsound loan portfolios.[13] Partly this is because of the loss of certain assets resulting from the break-up of the FSU (e.g., the Saving Bank). Partly it is due to state policy which directed these banks to make loans to enterprises even though they were not creditworthy (see Box 5.4). As interest rates are increased and more client enterprises become unprofitable, the problem of non-performing loan will get more serious.

At this stage, too little is known to develop a general solution to the problem of non-performing loans. The dimensions are unclear, and given the changes in interest rates and relative prices that are taking place and will take place in the near future, the picture is likely to worsen. In other countries where financial sector reform has been undertaken, it has involved recapitalization of the banks by exchanging government bonds for non-performing loans. And once recapitalized, banks have been corporatized (and subsequently privatized) to ensure that there are adequate incentives for owners and managers to lend only to creditworthy clients.

For this kind of solution to work, however, it is important to also simultaneously address the root cause of the problem, that is the behavior of enterprises. If this is not done, then it is likely that the problem of non-performing loans will recur. This is especially important because typically state enterprises are the major shareholders of banks, thus making it difficult for the bank to reject credit applications from its owner-clients. That is why restructuring of banks should be done in parallel with enterprise restructuring and privatization. At this stage, problem banks should be downsized. Subsequently, any recapitalization through the budget should be made conditional on the adoption of privatization and/or restructuring plans by the banks and by those enterprises responsible for the bad loans.

Prudential Regulations. Improved credit allocation depends also on having effective prudential regulations and a capacity to supervise the banks. The combination of de-facto if not de-jure deposit insurance and informational asymmetries creates the possibilities of fraud and non-competitive behavior.[14]

The mandate for bank supervision is provided by the laws "On Banks and Banking Activities", and "On the National Bank". A Banking Supervision division, with a staff of five, was created in early 1992 within the NBG. The main task of the division are licensing of the private commercial banks and analyzing their monthly reported balance sheets to monitor compliance with prudential regulations. On-site inspections are carried out by the Auditing department of the NBG, which is also responsible for monitoring the state commercial banks. However, effective banking supervision is difficult because the information and accounting system in banks is too poor to provide a good assessment of the quality of the bank's portfolio. Supervision capacity is also weak and will have to be considerably strengthened. A capacity also needs to be created to assess the performance of banks and their exposure in different sectors.

A big problem is the rapid proliferation of banks in the past one year. There are already more than 70 new private commercial banks. Despite their large numbers, as of mid-1992 these banks accounted for only 12 percent of the total short term credits extended in the economy and only 20 percent of total enterprise deposits. The banks are mostly owned by groups of enterprises that get loans from the bank they have established at favorable interest rates. Many of these banks exist only to borrow from the NBG,[15] and to use these low cost resources to subsidize lending to their owner-clients. This situation not only diverts financial resources to inefficient enterprises; the incestuous relationship between owners and clients undermines financial discipline and is a source of financial instability.

Licensing requirements need to be strengthened to make it more difficult to establish a bank. In the current law the maximum individual shareholding is 35 percent, which is higher than in many countries. The maximum shareholding limit should be lowered to 10-20 percent of capital. The minimum capital required to set up a bank (recently increased to Rbl 5 million for cooperative banks and to Rbl 20 million for private banks) is low by international standards and should be increased (to the equivalent of $1-2 million, at the market exchange rate). To enable banks to adjust to these standards, they may be given up to a year to adjust. The licensing fee should also be increased significantly. In addition, the financial and managerial standards required of founders of banks should be raised, at least to ensure that enterprises in financial difficulties (e.g., in arrears) cannot set up a bank. Licensing to conduct foreign exchange operations also need to be tightened.

Commercial banks are required to comply with five prudential regulations which aim at ensuring capital adequacy, risk division and liquidity. However, prudential regulations do not apply to state banks. With these banks accounting for 85 percent of total credit in the system, it is necessary that a program be adopted to enforce the compliance of state banks with the existing regulations. Of these regulations, the one most problematic is on risk division. The maximum credit given to any one client is required to be less than 50 percent of the paid in capital; and if the client is one of the founders of the bank, the loan cannot exceed 30 percent of the capital. These requirements are too weak: just two large borrowers could make the bank insolvent if their loans became uncollectible. It would be desirable to lower the limit to 15-20 percent of capital. A system of syndicated loans could be developed later to accommodate large borrowers.

The Payment System

The existing payment system is outdated and inefficient, and there are large delays in the execution of payment orders: it is estimated that the period between debiting of the sending bank and the crediting of the receiving bank in the books of the NBG may be as long as three weeks. In early January

1992, the float amounted to Rbl 17 billion in the Tbilisi center alone. The IMF has made several useful suggestions to improve the efficiency of the payment mechanism in the short term. These include: centralizing correspondent accounts in Tbilisi; use of cassettes or diskettes; use of couriers, etc.. Improvements that should be introduced over the medium term have also been suggested, including the development of a new communication infrastructure; the use of non-cash based payment systems, etc..

Accounting and Auditing

There are major discrepancies between the existing (Soviet) accounting rules and international standards. Work must be initiated to develop an accounting system that can provide relevant information to assess the state of the financial system and to identify problem areas. The IMF is assisting the government in reforming the accounting framework for the NBG. Subsequently, an action plan to prepare the transition to an internationally acceptable accounting framework for commercial banks will have to be developed. Equally important, specialized training for bank accountants and controllers will be necessary.

Training

The transition to markets will imply a significant change in the functions of the NBG and the commercial banks. The former will shift increasingly towards monetary policy and exchange rate management and supervision of banks, while commercial banks will have greater autonomy in credit allocation. An extensive training program will be required if this transformation is to be carried out successfully. Of particular importance is training in commercial bank management and operations, international accounting standards, credit evaluation, liability and asset management, interest rate management, analysis of client and enterprise accounts, foreign operations, trade finance, etc..

Endnotes

1. These include: law about privatization of state-owned enterprises (August 1991); law about bases of entrepreneurship (August 1991); law about free transition of dwelling (February 1992); decree concerning sale by auction (May 1992); decree about competitive sale or conditional auction (May 1992); regulation concerning the valuation of objects of privatization (August 1992); decree concerning the commercialization and transformation of enterprises into joint-stock companies (May 1992); and the Bankruptcy law (September 1992).

2. In Poland, for example, within 12-18 months, more than 80 percent of retail shop and small services had been privatized. In Hungary, in spite of avoidable delays, about 850 small retail trade and catering units were sold within 6-9 months of the enactment of the enabling law. In Czechoslovakia, about 16,500 units were auctioned off within a year after the privatization law was adopted. Source: Enterprise Reform in Central and Eastern Europe: Kochav and Sood, July 1992.

3. Employees may have a right of first refusal over their small firms. Should they choose not to buy, they may be awarded 20 months salary from the proceeds of the sale (this decision is not final). These preferences may not be completely unjustified since many of the managers and staff of small firms have invested their own capital in the maintenance and improvement of the enterprises.

4. The final decisions on large privatization has not yet been made. What is presented here reflects the expectations of officials of the SPM and the draft program.

5. One way this may be done is the following: Based upon a preliminary screening of enterprises that are good candidates for privatization (including supportive management, minimum worker resistance, availability or reliable enterprise data, favorable market condition, etc), the SPM could canvass potential investor interest and invite competitive offers for enterprises where there is demand. Sales could then be negotiated with the highest bidder. Where there is limited or no investor demand, the SPM could identify the reasons for lack of investor demand, and explore whether or not restructuring, partial divesture or other measures, such as lease, management contract or franchised production or distribution of products or services might enhance the attractiveness of those firms, or serve as an initial step toward eventual complete divesture. In this manner, the Georgian program might avoid the mistake of other countries, which have often invested considerable time and scarce financial and human resources in the identification, valuation and preparation for sale of selected public enterprises, in the often unfounded expectation that they would be of interest to potential buyers.

6. Thus for example the NBG subsidizes Georgian enterprises by maintaining its refinance rates lower than the rate of interest on refinancing credits from the Russian Central Bank. This subsidy is ultimately financed by depositors (who get low interest rates on their deposits) or by investors who do not have access to refinance credits (mostly the private sector). In the second half of 1992, credit to non-financial public enterprises expanded fourfold.

7. The 34 percent increase in the stock mainly resulted from the "compensation" provided to depositors in March 1991. A 40 percent bonus was granted to depositors to compensate them for the liberalization of prices. The corresponding amount, roughly Rbl 3 billion was initially supposed to be frozen in a special account for three years, but in June it was decided to credit these to the savers.

8. Not surprisingly, most of the lending by the three specialized state banks in the first six months of 1992 was based on refinancing credits from the NBG. Total credits extended by the three banks in the period

was about Rbl 11.6 billion, while deposits increased by only Rbl 1.5 billion. The difference was financed by the NBG through its refinancing loans.

9.   But for the Savings Bank, there is effectively a 100 percent reserve requirement. Reserves do not yield any interest.

10.   This applies only to lending by the specialized state banks; with some exceptions, private commercial banks currently do not have access to refinancing credits from the NBG. Banks are free to lend wherever and at whatever terms they want out of their own resources. However, lending by the specialized banks constituted the bulk of credit expansion in 1992.

11.   In 1991, these priorities were: (i) energy purchases, including electricity to restart the subway, gas from Turkmenistan, and gasoline imports; (ii) food supply, including purchase of grains, butter, sugar and vegetable oil; (iii) reactivation of important industrial plant, including the auto plant at Kutaisi and the chemical plant at Rustavi; and (iv) credit for agricultural planting season. The usual final recipient of the loan was a state enterprise.

12.   The interest rate on refinancing credits from the NBG was raised from 20 percent in January 1992 to 50 percent in June. It was subsequently reduced to 40 percent. These rates are considerably lower than the refinancing rate of the CBR of 80 percent. In addition, in late 1992 the NBG began a new policy of providing credit at even more preferential rates (10-30 percent) for "productive purposes". Of the total credit increase of Rbl 37 billion to enterprises in December 1992, at least Rbl 8 billion was at preferential rates.

13.   It is estimated that at the beginning of 1992 the ratio of non-performing short term loans to total short term loans was 11 percent. But the problem may be more severe: enterprises may be paying back the banks, but only by not paying other enterprises. There has been a large increase in arrears, from Rbl 3.2 billion at the end of 1991 to Rbl 20.6 billion by December 1, 1992.

14.   The Monetary and Exchange Affairs Department of the IMF has made detailed suggestions to improve the prudential regulations. This discussion draws on these recommendations. Source: IMF (August 1992).

15.   Though they were denied access to NBG financing during the first five months of 1992.

CHAPTER 6

Reform of the Social Safety Net

Introduction

In terms of social indicators, Georgia's condition is satisfactory. Primary and secondary school enrollment are high, illiteracy does not exist, life expectancy is the highest among countries of the former Soviet Union (except Latvia), health services are accessible. Social indicators are similar if not better than in countries of Europe with similar levels of per capita income (Table 1.2, Statistical Appendix). Income distribution is fairly compressed (see Box 6.1). A strong private and informal economy, and a tradition of close family ties served to maintain a relatively well off standard of living. This favorable condition was a direct result of policies of the previous system, which combined low salaries with widespread subsidization of essential products, including food, rent and energy; almost full coverage of the population by the state pension system, free health and education; and high participation rates for women.

With the deterioration in the overall economic situation, which began in the last five years, this favorable picture is beginning to show signs of strain. Social tensions can reach crisis proportions unless significant reforms are initiated in the social policies to deal effectively with the emerging problems. First, the decline in real incomes that has already occurred and is likely to continue for the next couple of years will push more and more people into poverty. Health and education standards of the population are also likely to deteriorate as the imperative of fiscal stringency will require cuts in public expenditures on social programs. Moreover, significant unemployment will emerge as economic restructuring gets under way. To deal with these new -- systemic -- issues, the existing apparatus of social protection will have to change. The most important concerns include: (i) how to deal with poverty which is expected to increase in the short term; (ii) how to protect the living standards of the pensioners and disabled population, especially those with low incomes; and (iii) how to assist those that are temporarily unemployed and empower them to find new jobs. This chapter deals with these issues.

Poverty And Its Alleviation

Awareness of poverty in Georgia is recent and was triggered by the earthquake in 1991 and the ethnic strife that produced several thousands of refugees. The only agency that deals with poverty is the Fund for Social Affairs set up within the Ministry of Labor, Social Protection and Demography after the earthquake at the end of 1991. Its original function was to distribute foreign aid to the victims of the earthquake. Its functions had since expanded to include social assistance to refugees fleeing the areas affected by the conflict, and aid to the poor in general. The Fund is extremely short of money to meet even the elementary needs of refugees.[1]

Estimates of the number of poor are highly uncertain and vary widely depending upon the definition of the poverty threshold and the purpose which such a definition is supposed to serve. Thus, based on some rough criteria using the minimum wage as the benchmark and excluding pensioners, the Fund for Social Affairs estimates the number of poor at 140,000 people, which is 2.5 percent of the population. Using a more appropriate (and higher) poverty threshold, close to the one adopted in Russia, results in classifying about 30 percent of the population as poor in 1990.[2] The poverty gap in 1990 (the amount needed to bring all the poor to the level of the poverty threshold) is estimated at 5.5 percent of the total income of the population, or between 3-3.5 percent of GDP. The gap (measured as a share of GDP) has widened since, both because of a further reduction in real incomes of the population and the decline in GDP. Assuming (very conservatively) a 30 percent decrease in real incomes across the board, the proportion of poor jumps to 60 percent of the population while the poverty gap increases to 13.3 percent of GDP.

Recommendations. It is difficult to see how such a large gap, higher than total pension payments, could be financed in present circumstances. Indeed, the prospect of continuing decline in economic activity, continuing armed conflict, and the need to maintain tight limits on budgetary expenditures make it very unlikely that **any** universal social assistance program, for almost any meaningful level of social minimum, is affordable at this time.

Consequently, to the extent possible, other mechanisms that already exist should take care of the poor. These include: (a) the Labor Fund, by paying unemployment benefits for 6-12 months; (b) family allowances, by alleviating poverty among children; and (c) growing private sector, both formal and informal, which should provide opportunities for gainful occupation. The extended family system will continue to play an important role in cushioning the impact of the transition, and with the progressive privatization of agriculture its role may become even more important.

Foreign financial assistance needs to be mobilized to meet the plight of the refugees and the poor. The greatest effort should therefore be directed toward informing various governmental and non-governmental foreign organization of their condition. At the same time, much better accounting for the use of foreign aid, and formation of a better network of local organizations should be the main priorities of the authorities. At present, rules according to which cash and in-kind assistance is given are almost entirely discretionary.[3] Clear criteria, such as, for example, granting cash aid only to refugees, or not giving aid to those possessing certain consumer durables, should be established and publicized. Increased transparency and tighter management of social assistance, combined with better information regarding who are the most vulnerable, should help mobilize more substantial inflows of foreign resources to assist the government in fighting poverty.

Pensions and Family Allowances

Pensions, family allowances and medical expenses (sick pay) are administered by the Unified Pension and Medical Insurance Fund.[4] The Fund is financed by a 37 percent payroll tax paid by both state-owned and private enterprises, plus 1 percent nominally paid by the employees. Budget institutions (schools, hospitals, state administration etc.) pay a 26 percent payroll tax, plus 1 percent paid by the employees.[5] The average rate of contribution is exactly the same as in Russia (31.6 percent for pensions plus 5.4 percent for family allowances, sick pay etc). Georgia's rate is also broadly in line with statutory payroll taxes for the same types of insurance in eastern Europe (Hungary 53 percent, Czechoslovakia 50 percent, Poland 43 percent) or continental western Europe (Italy 47 percent, France 46 percent, Germany about 40 percent). The rate is, however, substantially higher than in the UK and the United States (less than 20 percent of the wage bill) or in countries at approximately Georgia's GDP per capita level (Turkey 33 percent, Peru and Colombia 20 percent).[6]

Box 6.1
Income Distribution in Georgia

Income inequality in Georgia is about average by the Soviet standards: it is less than in Central Asian republics, higher than in Russia. The Gini coefficient for urban households is 24.4, and for rural households a slightly higher 25.4. The shape of the income distribution curve for Georgia (for all households) is contrasted in the figure with that for Hungary and the UK. Differences in the shape of income distribution between Hungary and Georgia are very small despite important differences in the level of income and structure of employment (note, however, higher share of top income decile in Hungary). What stands out in the comparison of Hungary and Georgia with the UK is relatively high share of the lowest income deciles (the lowest income decile in Hungary and Georgia receives 4.5 percent of total income vs. 2.8 percent in the UK) and relatively low share of the highest decile.

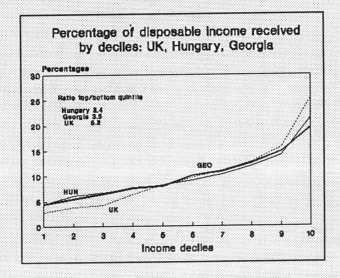

The problem is that while expenditures on pensions, family allowance and medical expenses are quite large, amounting in 1991 to Rbl 2.7 billion or 11.5 percent of GDP (see below), revenues to finance these expenditures are diminishing. As of mid-1992, receipts were only 50-60 percent of what was expected. This shortfall is due to several reasons: (i) some enterprises simply ignore the rules and do not contribute to the Fund; (ii) others do not pay because they do not have the money; (iii) some enterprises are practically shut down (due to civil war or shortage of inputs) and both their production and wage bill are nil; finally, (iv) the money from enterprises that do pay the tax may not always reach the Fund because banks lack rubles and fail either to remit the money to the Fund or to pay beneficiaries when requested by the Fund. Revenues from Southern Ossetia are also not being received due to the armed conflict there. As a result, pensions and sick leave compensations are not being paid regularly. Unless reforms are introduced to reduce the claims on the Fund, by revising the system and tightening eligibility, and increased efforts made to collect revenues owed to the Fund, payment of pension and other benefits from the Fund would become a chronic problem. The necessary reforms are discussed below.[7]

Pensions

Pension expenditures (for old age, disability, survivor's, and social pensions) account for roughly 10 percent of GDP in Georgia. This share is quite high compared to most east European countries and is closer to the average in developed western countries (Table 6.1). The high share of pensions in GDP is explained by: (i) a relatively large share of population receiving pensions (21 percent of the population receive some type of pension). This ratio is similar to what is found in the other countries of the FSU, except the Central Asian Republics whose population is relatively young, and (ii) pensions are also relatively high compared to wages: in 1991 the ratio between the average pension and the average state-sector wage was 70 percent. This compares with 53 percent for east and central European countries, and 55 percent for the developed western economies.

GEORGIA
Table 6.1
Pensioners and Pensions in Selected Countries

	Pensioners as % of population	Pensions as % of GDP	Pension as % of wage[a]	Pensioners as % of employed
Austria	21.2	12.8	68	
Former West Germany		11.8	49	
France		12.3	66	
Italy	28	8.3	69	
United Kingdom	24[b]	9.5	31	
United States	23[b]	8.2	44	
Average	**24**	**10.5**	**55**	
Hungary	24.2	8.5	67	
Poland	18.6	8.0	55	
Czechoslovakia	26.5	10.0	49	
Bulgaria	20.2	6.6	47	
Romania	14.6	5.7	47	
Average	**20.8**	**7.8**	**53**	
Russia	22.8	8		7.7
Ukraine	25.2	13.0		7.3
Belarus	23.1			7.4
Armenia	16.3			8.4
Kazakhstan	18.0	4.7	39	4.5
Estonia	22.6	5.6	33	12.2
Average	**21.3**			**7.9**
Georgia	**21.0**	**9.8**	**70**	**12.3**

a/ Average state sector wage for non-market economies.

b/ Number of recipients of occupational and private pensions is estimated based on the share of occupational and private pensions in total pensions.

Pension recipients. For Poland (year 1990), Czechoslovakia (1989), Bulgaria (1989), and Hungary (1990) from country's statistical yearbooks. For the former Soviet Union (beginning of 1991), data from *Narodnoe khozyaystvo SSSR v 1990 godu*, Moscow, 1991, p.76, except for Kazakhstan (1992), Country Economic Memorandum, World Bank, July 1992, Report No. 10976-KK, vol.1, p. 111; and Estonia, "The Transition to a Market Economy", Country Economic Report, July 6, 1992, p.119. For Romania (1990), *Human Resources and the Transition to a Market Economy*, World Bank Country Study, 1992, Tables 3.1 (p.177), 3.3 (p.179). For the US, from US Department of Health and Human Services SSA, *A Brief Description of the US Social Security Program*, 1992, p.1 and *Statistical Abstract of the United States 1990*, pp. 361-2 and 367; UK: Department of Social Security, *Social Security Statistics 1991*, Table B1.04. Austria: *Statistisches Handbuch 1991*, Table 9.14, p.153. Pensions as share of GDP. Data for market economies from Esping-Andersen, The *Three Worlds of Welfare Capitalism*, Princeton: Princeton University Press, 1990, p. 84. Data for 1980. For socialist economies (except Romania) own calculations. Romania: op. cit. For Kazakhstan, Estonia, op. cit., Ukraine: "Employment, Social Protection, and Social Spending in the Transition to a Market Economy", Report No. 11176-UA, October 1992, pp. 79. Pensions and wages. For East European countries, statistical yearbooks. Kazakhstan, op. cit, vol.1, p. 112, and vol.2, Table 8.5. Estonia, op. cit. For OECD countries, OECD, *Reforming Public Pensions*, OECD: Paris, 1988, p.50 (quoted from I. Rutkowska, "Public Transfers in Socialist and Market Economies", Social Expenditures and their Distributional Impact Project, Paper No.7, Socialist Economies Reform Unit, World Bank, 1991). Pensioners as percentage of the employed: From *Narodnoe Khozyaystvo SSSR v 1988 godu*, Moscow, 1989, p.45. Data for the year 1987.

Disability pensioners and working pensioners (people who work although they receive a pension) account for almost 40 percent of all pensioners, and 8 percent of Georgia's population (Table 6.2). Indeed, of all the republics of the former Soviet Union, Georgia has the highest percentage of working pensioners among the employed. Old age pensioners account for 49 percent of all pensioners (and 11 percent of the population).

GEORGIA
Table 6.2
Number of Pensioners and Monthly Amounts of Pensions (in Rbl)

	1991 Number of recipients	1991 Pension Amount	1992 (January - April) Pension Amount
Old-age pensions	557,328	169	418
Disability pens.	163,000	181	
-job-related	15,000	192	424
-general	148,000	180	400
Survivor's pens.	64,000	147	334
Working pensioners	275,600	167	374
Total	1,145,000	167	380
Memo:			
Employment/Average Wage[a]	2,300,000	227	550
Minimum wage	n.a.	n.a.	500[b]
Minimum pension	n.a	n.a.	420[b]

Note: The data for the first 4 months of 1992 are preliminary.
[a] Includes cooperative farmers and state-sector employees outside agriculture.
[b] June 1992.

Men receive full old-age pensions at 60 years of age and after 25 years of paid contributions. Women receive their full pensions at 55, and after 20 years of paid contribution. The formula according to which pensions are calculated is simple: the pension is equal to 55 percent of the worker's wage, where the wage is defined as the average wage in the last year or in the last five years (whichever is more favorable). In calculating the pension, past wages are indexed for inflation. At the time of retirement, therefore, pensions simply reflect past wages. However, a *flat* amount is normally added to all existing pensions to compensate for increases in the cost of living.[8] In the first four months of 1992, the average pension was Rbl 380, or about 70 percent of the average state-sector wage.[9] In June 1992, the minimum pension was Rbl 420, that is 16 percent below the minimum wage.

Disability pensions are paid according to the type of disability and years of service. No individual circumstances are taken into account, that is no attempt is made to determine the actual loss of earning potential for the individual. Disability pensions are of two types: for job-related injuries and general disability. The pension rules for the former type are more favorable. Apparently disability pensions are granted relatively frequently (the ratio between the number of disability and old-age pensioners is almost 1 to 3, and among the disability pensioners, general disability pensioners predominate). Disability pensions are relatively generous: in 1991, disability pensions were, on average, higher than the old-age pensions (Table 6.2).

A special category of pensioners are working pensioners. These are people who have qualified for old-age pension, receive the pension, but continue to work. Like in other socialist countries, this category is fairly numerous. Since 1990 their number is decreasing because of a new regulation according to which pension and wage must not exceed Rbl 1500 (about 3.5 minimum pensions). Some pensioners have therefore given up their pensions to receive wages in excess of Rbl 1500, while others may have decided to quit working as the wage they were allowed to receive was very small. Social pensions are paid to all men (women) of 65 (60) years of age who do not qualify for any other type of pension. Social pension is equal to the minimum pension. There is no income test.

Recommendations. As mentioned earlier, expenditures on pensions are typically less in other countries at the same per capita income level as Georgia (Table 6.1). Georgia has a large number of pensioners, and among them the number of working pensioners and those receiving disability pensions are particularly large. Efforts to reduce expenditure on pensions must address these two groups.

The category of working pensioners should be either discontinued or strongly discouraged. The steps already taken have resulted in some decrease in their numbers (from 400,000 in 1990 to about 300,000 in 1992). This should be continued. Two different approaches can be adopted. The present ceiling on the combined amount of pension and wage (Rbl 1500 as of mid 1992) can be retained or increased very slowly. With the passage of time, more and more people will have to decide either to take a pension or a wage. A second approach would be to discontinue the category of working pensioners immediately by requiring the recipients to choose between wage and pension.[10] Under the first approach, some expenditures on working pensioners will remain although probably not for very long if the ceiling is not raised or is raised substantially less than the rate of inflation. Under the second approach, expenditures on working pensioners will cease.

The decisions on granting disability pensions are not based on estimated loss of earning capacity of the individual but on whether a particular disease is considered *in general* to be associated with lower work ability. The eligibility criteria for general disability pensions should be made much more restrictive by reducing the number of injuries/maladies that give rise to disability pensions and by trying to estimate individualized loss of earning capacities with general losses serving as maximums.

The changes in the pension law being currently debated call for a five-year increase of the retirement age (to 65 years for men and 60 for women). Although such a decision may be politically unpopular, it is a sound one, particularly since life expectancy in Georgia is at par with that in many developed countries. However, some thought could be given to the possibility of equalizing retirement age for men and women choosing, for example, a median age of sixty-two.[11] The pension system should not be viewed as an instrument to address the unemployment problem. Attempts to do this by lowering of the retirement age should be resisted.

Family Allowances

There are various types of family (child and maternity) allowances. At each child's birth the mother receives Rbl 500 (equal to a monthly minimum wage). The Fund also pays 100 percent of the mother's last month's wage, indexed for inflation, for 126 days. During the subsequent 18 months, the Fund pays to the mother a flat amount (currently Rbl 300); this amount is afterwards lowered to Rbl 250 per month till the child is 6 years old. Throughout these six years, single mothers receive an additional Rbl 250 per month.[12]

Recommendations. Most of the family (children-related) allowances currently existing in Georgia should be retained (including the child allowance paid at birth). This should be done for two reasons. First, such allowances are generally well targeted on the poor families because of a strong negative relationship between the number of children and household's standard of living.[13] Secondly, children, who are future citizens and workers of Georgia, should be spared as much as possible the worst pain of the current economic adjustment. This is not purely a social but also an economic argument because impairment at an early age translates later into lower education attainment and productivity.

Sick Leave

Unlike in many other countries, where sick leave is partly paid by the employer and partly by the Social Security Fund, sick leave in Georgia is paid out entirely by the Fund. Since enterprises are not bearing any of the cost of sick leave, it could be expected that they may encourage workers to resort to sick leave in order to reduce their wage bill and all other taxes attached to the payroll.[14] A worker is entitled to sick pay for up to 5 months per year (4 months at most continuously) and with doctor's certificate. The sick pay scale varies in function of worker's seniority in the state-sector (regardless of his/her service in a particular enterprise). If seniority is less than 5 years, the worker is entitled to 60 percent of last month's wage; between 5 and 8 years of seniority, to 80 percent of the wage, and to a full wage with more than 8 years of seniority.[15]

Recommendations. The level of the benefit and the duration (up to 5 months) is simply too generous. The payment schedule should depend on the length of the sick leave rather than on seniority. The compensation for the first week, in addition to being paid by the firms, should be less (say, 80 percent of the wage) in order to discourage frequent taking of leave. Moreover, the average number of days of sick leave in most economies (market and non-market) ranges between 15 and 20 per year. The number of paid sick leave days should therefore be reduced.

A larger share of sick leave payments should be borne by enterprises. They must bear the cost for at least the first week of sick leave. This is necessary so that enterprises do not encourage workers to fake sick leave in order to shift a portion of their short term operational costs to the state.

Unemployment Compensation

Unemployment is becoming a major issue in Georgia. The number of unemployed rose to 116,000 (5.4 percent of labor force) by December 1992 from only 61,000 (2.8 percent of labor force) in June 1992. Though mass lay-offs have not started yet, it is estimated that a large number of employees were on long term unpaid leave from their enterprises. Both the financing and the legal framework regarding eligibility for unemployment benefits, replacements rates etc. are in place. Two institutions deal with unemployment: the off-budget Labor Fund, which was founded in June 1991, and whose primary functions are disbursement of unemployment benefits and retraining of redundant workers; and the State Labor Exchange, whose primary function is matching of workers' skills with available vacancies (informational function).[16]

The Labor Fund is financed out of a 3 percent wage tax paid by state-owned and private enterprises.[17] As mentioned previously in the context of social insurance contributions, actual inflows are much less than what they should be, because many enterprises fail to pay the tax. "Normal" revenues from the wage tax for the period June 1991-June 1992 should have been between Rbl 750 and Rbl 900 million: actual revenues were only Rbl 51 million. In addition to revenues from the wage tax, the Fund has some (though minimal) income from two factories that it operates (a tile and a textile factory). In 1991, the Fund received a budgetary transfer of Rbl 7 million. No budget subsidy was received in 1992.

In theory at least, unemployment compensation is generous. Benefits extend for a period of 12 months.[18] In 1992, the payment schedule was as follows: for the first 3 months, 100 percent of the wage; for the next 4-6 months, 70 percent; during the following 7-9 months, 50 percent; and in the 10-12 months, the minimum wage.[19] This yields an average replacement rate for the year as a whole of about 65 percent which is in the upper ranges of the ratios in Eastern and Western Europe (Table 6.3).[20] People released from jails, mental hospital and the Army as well as the first-time job entrants are eligible for benefits. Initially, their benefits equal the minimum wage, and then decrease gradually. Attendance of retraining classes is not a requirement and no difference in payments schedules exists between those who attend retraining courses and those who do not. Benefits during the first three months are paid by the enterprise, and the rest by the Fund.

In addition to its "core" functions (registering the unemployed and administering the benefit system), the Fund organizes retraining, some job matching etc, provides in-kind help for the unemployed, and pays out

GEORGIA
Table 6.3
Unemployment Benefits

	Duration (in months)	Replacement Rate (period average)
Austria	3-7	50-70
France	3-26	57-75
Germany	12-22	63-68
United Kingdom	12	33[a]
Poland	12	50
Czechoslovakia	12	50
Hungary	12	65
Romania	6	50-60
Armenia	7	56
Russia	12	56
Georgia	**12**	**65**

Sources: Market and East European economies CECSE data base except for Romania: *Human Resources and the Transition to Market Economy*, World Bank Country Study, 1992, pp.61 and 73, and the UK: Deakin and Wilkonson, "Labour Law, Social Security and Economic Inequality", Cambridge Journal of Economics, June 1991, p. 125. Armenia: M. Vodopivec, "Labor Market Issues", mimeo, 1992. Russia: T. King, "Policy Discussions on the Social Safety Net-A Progress Report", mimeo, July 20, 1992, p.9.

a/ For a married worker with two children earning average wage.

wage subsidies to selected enterprises. The Fund thus pays for teachers' salaries, rent of the classrooms and other expenses involved in workers' retraining. Recently, the Fund began to provide the unemployed with meat, milk and other food at some 40 percent of the market price. It also plans to open soup kitchens for the unemployed. Finally, the Fund gives interest-free loans to enterprises that commit to preserve jobs. The criteria for such subsidies are unclear. Of particular concern is the fact that over the last 12 months ending in June 1992, the Fund's expenditures for job subsidies were not much less than expenditures on unemployment benefits.[21] Although the number of the "saved" jobs is unknown, it is quite possible that the cost per "saved" job may be very high, much higher than the cost of providing unemployment compensations.

Those who have voluntarily left their job and thus do not have the status of the registered unemployed may be registered with the Labor Exchange. They register either because they expect to find a new job more easily through the Exchange (the Exchange provides information on vacancies and organizes retraining courses at its Professional Orientation Institutes) or because they receive some small benefits. In mid-1992 the benefits included Rbl 40 per month as compensation for the removal of bread subsidy.[22] They can also use a free health polyclinic run by the Labor Exchange.

Despite the generous benefits afforded to the unemployed, so far the Fund's expenditures have been very limited. This is mainly due to three reasons. First, large scale job losses have only just started. Second, many people who are unemployed do not even know that they are entitled to benefits. This is particularly the case for the first-time job entrants who are eligible for the minimum wage during the first 3 months. Third, only the registered unemployed have the right to benefits. To be registered a person must have lost the job due to downsizing and must be willing to work.[23] Also, benefits are discontinued if the individual refuses two job offers deemed adequate by the Fund. In 1992, only 10.5 percent of the unemployed workers (5.4 percent of the labor force by end 1992) received benefits.

As in the case of pensions, expenditures on unemployment compensation have also been severely constrained by the lack of rubles. As a result, many benefits are overdue. Outlays on unemployment benefits in the first six months of 1992 amounted to only Rbl 6 million. The average unemployment benefit in June 1992 was only Rbl 300 (60 percent of the minimum wage).[24]

Recommendations. While expenditures from the Fund are low now, this situation is likely to change rapidly if economic reforms are implemented with vigor and restructuring gets under way. As the number of unemployed increase, and as more and more of them register as unemployed, the pressure on the finances of the Labor Fund will grow. Unless the existing entitlements are modified, financing these entitlements will entail further increasing the tax burden on enterprises. Indeed, if present benefits levels are maintained, and if unemployment occurs as it did in Poland or Slovakia, then the current payroll tax revenues (based on a 3 percent wage tax) will not be sufficient to cover unemployment expenditures after the first year of stabilization. The wage tax would have to increase in the second year to at least 3.8 if unemployment emerges as it did in Poland, and to 4.6 percent if the unemployment pattern is like in Slovakia (Table 6.4).[25] This increase can only be avoided by reducing and streamlining the administration of entitlements, and/or by utilizing savings from other programs.

Put in another way, the calculations suggest that in order not to increase the payroll tax above 3 percent, current entitlements will have to be drastically reduced: by about a third, from the annual replacement ratio of 65 percent to 40 percent for Poland-type unemployment, and by even more if the emerging pattern of unemployment is like in Slovakia. These reductions are too much and would only increase poverty. A more moderate reduction in benefits, combined with some additional taxation, or additional financing from other sources, may be the only way out.

The replacement ratio may most easily be reduced to a little over 50 percent (which is probably the minimum rate below which individuals would fall into extreme poverty) by lowering the benefits during the first three months of unemployment from the present level of 100 percent (paid by the enterprises) to 70 percent (paid by the Fund)[26]; by reducing benefits in the next two quarters to 60 percent and 50 percent of the previous wage respectively; and by maintaining the minimum wage during the last quarter.

GEORGIA

Table 6.4

Financing of Unemployment Benefits: A Simulation with Current Unemployment Entitlements

Pattern in the Increase of Unemployment

	Polish	CSFR	Slovak 1	Slovak 2 [c]
Year One				
End-year unemployment (000)	207	195	320	320
End-year % of unemployed	8.3	7.8	12.8	12.8
Take-up rate [a]	37.3	35.0	37.5	69.9
Benefit as % average wage [b]	56.2	55.0	56.9	56.9
Year Two				
End-year unemployment (000)	345	172	325	
End-year % of unemployed	13.8	6.9	13.0	
Take-up rate [a]	69.2	70.1	70.3	
Benefit as % average wage [b]	42.4	40.5	38.2	
Required payroll tax (%)	**3.8**	**2.5**	**4.6**	

[a] Average yearly rate.

[b] At the year-end

[c] Slovak 2 is the same as Slovak 1 except for a higher take-up rate.

Note: In all simulations it is assumed that the average wage of those who are laid-off is equal to 80 percent of state-sector average wage. The latter is the numeraire.

Currently unemployment benefits are also paid to the people released from jails, the Army, and new job entrants. The benefits should be discontinued for all three groups, and most emphatically, for the first-time job entrants. Theoretically, unemployment benefits are a payment that depends on the worker's contribution during his active life (it is an insurance). Although in practice unemployment benefits are used to fulfill other social functions as well, they should not be viewed by the people leaving the school system as a right. The first-time job entrants should be encouraged to look after themselves and to try to find a job (even if it may be temporarily below their level of skill) as fast as possible.

Unemployment benefits may be claimed by casual workers employed in small private-sector firms. It is therefore important to make sure that workers, in order to become eligible for unemployment benefits, ought to have worked and paid their contribution for at least some minimum period (say, one year), and that the coverage includes only firms with 10 workers or more. This means that the minimum contribution record (presently 3 months) should be raised, and the smallest size of establishment covered by the unemployment insurance be explicitly stated.

The Labor Fund and Labor Exchange are currently engaged in activities they are not best suited to perform. These include providing wage subsidies to enterprises that maintain employment, financing of medical services to the unemployed, provision of low cost food etc. The Labor Fund should discontinue these tasks which may be performed, if necessary by other government bodies. The Fund and the Exchange should concentrate on disbursement of benefits, skill and job matching, and retraining.

With these changes in the current benefits, the payroll tax needs to be increased to only 3.2 percent (from the current 3 percent) to meet the Poland-type unemployment, and to 3.9 percent to meet the needs of the Slovakia-type on unemployment.[27] The increase in the tax rates would finance an additional spending on unemployment compensation equivalent to 0.1-0.4 percent of GDP.[28] However, it would be preferable to finance the increased demands for unemployment compensation without increasing the payroll taxes at all.[29] This can be done partly by reducing unemployment benefits, as outlined above, and by utilizing the savings from other programs, particularly by restricting pensions, as shown below.

Financial Implications of Recommendations

The proposed reforms in the pension and sick pay system are expected to yield savings that could be used for strengthening other social programs such as the unemployment compensation scheme, or for poverty alleviation. Tentative financial estimates of savings from changes in existing pension and sick pay programs, and the additional demand for resources due to increasing unemployment and poverty are presented in Table 6.5. All estimates are on annual basis, and refer to the second year of the government's stabilization and reform program.

The largest reduction in expenditures can be realized by the

GEORGIA
Table 6.5
Estimated financial effects of the recommendations
(in percent of GDP)

Fiscal savings

Fewer working pensioners	0.8-1
Increase of retirement age	0.2-0.25
Reduction in sick payments and fewer disability pensioners	0.3-0.4
Total	1.3-1.65

Use of savings

For additional unemployment expenditures */	0.1-0.4
For poverty alleviation	1.2-1.25

Poverty gap (1992)	**6.6-13.3**

Memo:

Poverty alleviation as fraction of poverty gap (%)	9-18

Note: */ Expenditures that cannot be financed from the existing payroll taxation.

Hypotheses used for the estimation explained in the text. Existing statutory tax rates assumed unchanged.

discouragement of simultaneous receipts of pensions and wages. Assuming that about one-third of working pensioners choose working instead of retiring, pension expenditures would be reduced by 8-10 percent or by equivalent of 0.8-1 percent of GDP.[30] A one-year increase in retirement age will probably cut the annual inflow of new pensioners in half (assuming that some newly disabled people or the already eligible do become pensioners). The annual rate of increase of pensioners would decrease from about 3 percent per year to 1.5 percent per year, generating savings equivalent to 0.2-0.25 percent of GDP. Tighter disability pension and sick pay requirements would reduce expenditures by a further 0.3-0.4 percent of GDP.[31] Taken together, the proposed reforms would result in savings between 1.3 and 1.65 percent of GDP.

These savings can be used to strengthen other social programs, and in particular to reduce poverty and/or provide relief to the unemployed. First, a part of the savings can be used to meet the increased demand for unemployment compensation: as shown above (para. 37), by transferring 0.1-0.4 percent of GDP for unemployment compensation, there will be no need to increase the existing payroll tax. The proposed reduction in unemployment benefits (so that replacement ratio declines from 65 percent to 50 percent) plus this transfer would be adequate to finance the increased demand from the unemployed.

Second, the rest of the savings should be directed toward poverty alleviation. It was estimated the poverty gap in 1992 would be about 13 percent of GDP. Even if the gap is half of that amount,[32] the remaining savings equivalent to 1.2 percentage point of GDP can fill at best about one-fifth of the needs. Although these figures are only rough estimates, the order of magnitudes involved shows that even under the optimistic scenario, the savings would fall far short of what is needed to fund a universal welfare scheme. The best that can be expected in the short-run is continued recourse to foreign funding and some ad-hoc help to the most destitute along the lines of what already exists (help for the refugees, food aid). In order to deliver such help more effectively, a denser network of local (community-based) institutions should be developed. However, if a universal welfare system is desired, the only alternative is a substantial increase in the already-high taxation.

Endnotes

1. According to some preliminary estimates done by the Fund, the amount needed to alleviate only the elementary needs of the refugees in 1992 is Rbl 650 million ($5.4 million at the June 1992 exchange rate). The Fund's 1992 request to the government was for one-fifth of that amount. Nothing, however, was received. The Fund's only source of funds is foreign donations and some past government grants.

2. Rbl 125 per month per capita (at 1990 prices) or about Rbl 2000 at mid-1992 prices. This is close to the Russian threshold of Rbl 2,150, which is appropriate given higher prices in Russia compared to Georgia.

3. Granting of aid seems to depend on the recipient's luck, perseverance, and, possibly, influence that he/she can wield with the authorities rather than on intrinsic merit of the case.

4. It also pays for funeral allowance and costs of treatment of invalids in state sanatoria. Health care is financed out of the general budget revenues. The Fund does not cover the whole territory of Georgia. There is a separate (and similarly organized fund) for the Autonomous Republic of Abkhazia.

5. Enterprises employing the handicapped pay only 10 percent payroll tax.

6. Data on statutory rates obtained from Social Security Programs Throughout the World-1989, US Department of Health and Human Services, Social Security Administration, Washington, D.C., May 1990.

7. So long as the political situation is unstable, enterprises fail to pay their taxes, and currency is in short supply, financial planning is impossible. In such conditions, no system can function. Changes which may be, theoretically, very good, are in practice meaningless. If systemic changes as well as the recommendations contained here are to have any meaning, it is necessary that the essential political prerequisites be in place (civic stability, ability of the government to collect taxes and to administer distribution of benefits). In discussing the affordability of social programs it is assumed that such conditions (return to normalcy) will be established soon.

8. Thus all pensions were raised by Rbl 100 per month on May 1, 1992. Similar flat increases were implemented in Fall 1992. With high inflation, these flat increases will become more and more important (compared to the original pension) and the difference between the pensions will decrease.

9. This share fell significantly during the rest of 1992. The ratio of the average pension to the average wage for the year was about 20 percent. The average minimum wage was also about 20-21 percent of the average wage in 1992.

10. This is already included among the proposals for reform of pensions.

11. The increase of the retirement age may take place gradually.

12. This represented the situation as of April 1992. Since then, there have been changes. Currently, the mother is paid Rbl 2000 when a child is born. During the next 18 months the Fund also pays the mother 60 percent of the minimum wage. This is lowered to 50 percent of the minimum wage per month until the child is 6 years old.

13. Family allowances are practically the only relatively important type of social transfers that are focussed on the poor in socialist economies. See B. Milanovic, "Distributional Incidence of Cash and In-Kind

Transfers in Eastern Europe and Russia", Socialist Economies Reform Unit, project Social Expenditures and their Distributional Impact in Eastern Europe, June 1992, Paper No. 9, pp. 14-5.

14.   As noted in Box 1.1, Georgia is noted for its high level of absenteeism.

15.   Sick pay is only irregularly indexed and replacement ratios are somewhat eroded.

16.   Labor Exchange also manages the disbursement of unemployment benefits through its 12 regional offices.

17.   Budget institutions are exempted from this tax.

18.   After that period, benefits are zero, and people may apply for social aid which is not universal nor guaranteed.

19.   Wage is defined as the average of the wage in the two last months prior to job loss. There are also caps on benefits. The caps are 3 and 2 times the minimum wage respectively for the periods between the 3rd and 9th month. All registered unemployed are at the minimum wage level after 9 months. Some people who have become unemployed earlier may receive less than the minimum wage because of benefits' irregular indexation.

20.   From November 1, 1992 unemployment benefits have been linked to the minimum wage rather than to the wage. For the first 3 months the benefit is 80 percent of the minimum wage; it goes down to 70 percent, 60 percent and 50 percent for each successive 3 months. The minimum monthly wage in November 1992 was Rbl 1700.

21.   Rbl 10.5 million for unemployment benefits and Rbl 7 million for job subsidies.

22.   The compensation for bread (paid to all registered unemployed not entitled to unemployment benefits) was raised several times from Rbl 10 per person per month in September 1992 to Rbl 680 in March 1993. In December 1992 the outlays on bread subsidies alone (Rbl 17 million) exceeded unemployment benefits (Rbl 11 million).

23.   Twice a month, he/she must check with Labor Exchange if there are job openings.

24.   The calculated average includes also individuals who, although entitled to benefits, received none because of ruble shortage.

25.   Indeed, if take-up rates increase quickly, which is not inconceivable given the low rate assumed in the simulation, the current tax would barely cover expenditures in the first year. If this were to happen, reforms to reduce entitlements would become even more urgent. Calculations, presented in Table 6.5, are derived under assumptions that: (a) take-up rate (percentage of the unemployed who claim benefits) increases in the first year of stabilization from the current level of 10 percent to about 70 percent, and stabilizes there in the second year, and (b) the increase in the number of the unemployed follows patterns recorded in Poland or Czechoslovakia, or Slovakia in their first two years of stabilization. The estimated rate of unemployment ranges for the first-year end between 7.8 percent and 12.8 percent of labor force. It then either declines (as in Czechoslovakia) or reaches between 13 and 14 percent as in Slovakia and Poland.

26.   The rationale for moving the payment of unemployment benefits from enterprises to the Fund, while shifting the payment of some sick leave compensations from the Fund back to enterprises, lies in attempts to delineate clearly the functions of enterprises and the state. The state should pay unemployment benefits

because premia for unemployment insurance are collected by the state. Enterprises should pay for a part of sick leave to avoid that short fake sick leaves are used to reduce short-term enterprises' operation costs by shifting them to the state. Compensation for longer, presumably legitimate diseases (longer and legitimate are related because diseases requiring longer leave are more difficult to fake) should, however, be paid by the state.

27. These are to be compared to the required payroll tax of 3.8 percent and 4.6 percent for Poland-type and Slovakia-type unemployment respectively in the absence of any reduction in unemployment benefits.

28. This is obtained from the fact that wages represent about 45-50 percent of GDP.

29. As already mentioned, even the existing payroll taxes are hard to collect. Increasing them will not necessarily raise more resources. Secondly, increasing the payroll tax will reduce the competitiveness of Georgian enterprises at a time when everything possible should be done to strengthen their competitiveness. Third, higher statutory rate of payroll taxation, even if introduced as a temporary measure, could easily prove permanent.

30. Since the wages/pensions ratio is expected to increase, even larger percentage could opt for employment. However, the number of available jobs may be reduced. Consequently, a rather conservative assumption is made that two-thirds of working pensioners continue to receive pensions.

31. This is based on shifting of part of sickness payments to the enterprises and about 20 percent reduction in the use of sick pay. Currently, sick pay is estimated at 5 percent of wages fund or about 2 percent of GDP.

32. Because the poverty line is probably too high.

ANNEX 1

The Industrial Sector[1]

Background

Prior to World War II, the industrial sector in Georgia was small, and concentrated in food processing, mining, light industries (particularly textiles), and woodworking. The major thrust of subsequent industrialization under the auspices of the Soviet central government focused primarily on rapid development of military production, and thereafter on electro-machinery building, and heavy industry. Industry accounted for about 39 percent of Net Material Product during 1989-91. The share fell to 34 percent in 1992.

Structure of Industry

Over the last two decades, there has been a large decline in relative importance of mining and metallurgy, while some new industries have emerged (machinery, chemicals and electronics) (Table A1.1). While the change towards non-traditional industries reflects the industrialization policy of the central Soviet authorities which gave high priority to such investments, it is interesting to note that Georgia succeeded in maintaining a high activity in food processing industry. Food industry accounted for about 40 percent of the industrial output in 1990 and 18 percent of industrial employment. The light industries are the second most important sector in terms of output (22 percent), followed by machine building and mechanical industry including production for military purposes (aviation). Electronics, which was developed more recently, is another significant subsector.

There are nearly 1365 state-owned industrial enterprises in Georgia (Table A1.2). Prior to independence, only about 65 percent of the industrial enterprises located in Georgia were effectively controlled by the Georgian Government[2]. Till enterprises are targeted for privatization, the Ministries of Industry, Construction and Food Processing retain responsibilities for their management (including the appointment of managers). Thereafter their ownership is transferred to the State Property Agency which is in charge of further privatization and corporatization (see Chapter 5).

Table A1.1
Development of the Industrial Sector[a]

	Share of Industrial Output			Share of Industrial Employment
	1970	1980	1990	1990
Food industry	35.9	35.2	39.9	17.5
Light industry	23.5	23.3	22.0	25.6
Machine building	9.2	11.7	15.1	29.5
Mining and metallurgy	10.4	6.2	3.7	5.5
Forest industries	3.2	3.4	3.4	6.7
Chemicals (incl. oil refining)	3.2	2.9	3.8	5.2
Building materials	5.1	5.2	5.3	10.1
Other (including electronics)	1.1	5.4	3.8	--

[a] Excluding electric power generation and fuel

Table A1.2
Enterprises and Employment in the Industrial Sector[a]

Industrial Branch	Number of Enterprises	Number of Employees	Average Employees per enterprise
Food industry	443	77,700	175
Light industry	246	114,000	453
Machine building	175	131,000	749
Mining and metallurgy	20	24,400	1,220
Forest industries	110	29,900	272
Chemicals	40	23,200	580
Building materials	146	44,500	305
Other	185	---	---
	1,365		

[a] Excluding electric power generation

Source: Ministry of Industry, Statistical Office

The principal characteristics of Georgian industries are:

Their large size. In common with the industrial structure in other parts of the former Soviet Union and the former CMEA counties (Poland, Hungary, Bulgaria etc), the average size of Georgian enterprises is large: it is around 370 employees compared, for example, with an average of 160 employees per industrial enterprise in the EC.[3]

Their monopolistic or oligopolistic nature. Until recently, a number of enterprises in machine building, including military were the main suppliers of components to the former Soviet Union. Examples abound: the Sukhoi fighter planes factory in Tbilisi was one of the two complexes producing fighter planes; the former "Lenin" electric locomotives factory in Tbilisi is one of the two factories of the FSU, and the only one producing DC locomotives; the Rustavi metallurgical amalgamation was producing 90 percent of the Soviet oil drilling tubes. Even in the light industries and in food processing, some enterprises organized into "Associations" had also a monopolistic or oligopolistic position in the Georgian domestic market, and even at ex-Union level (tea).

Production for military uses. A large share of production was for military uses, particularly in the machine building enterprises and also electronics.[4] The most famous factory was producing the Sukhoi fighters in Tbilisi.

A high degree of integration with Soviet industry, particularly in the machine building, chemical and electronic enterprises. The Georgian enterprises depended heavily on supplies of raw materials (metals, crude oil, basic chemicals, cotton, wool, etc) as well as parts and sub-assemblies from other parts of the Soviet Union. At the same time, most of the output of the industrial sector was exported to the other republics. Products from agroindustries and components for machines accounted for a substantial part of these exports.[5]

The almost exclusive ownership of the State. Until recently, there were only a handful of privately-owned industrial enterprises in Georgia. A few light industries and construction enterprises have taken the opportunity of "independence" when the Soviet Law on lease was passed in 1988, but they are in an awkward position until they are fully privatized. Most of the embryonic private initiative was concentrated on trade where quicker profits with a limited initial capital are possible.[6]

The large size of inventories. All enterprises have significant inventories of raw materials and parts. In addition to their own large inventories, most enterprises were in charge of strategic stockpiles and inventories financed and deposited by the Union to cover up to three months production in the event of war. These strategic stockpiles are now the property of the Government of Georgia.

Recent Performance

Industrial output decreased by 4.2 percent in 1990 and declined further by 20.7 percent in 1991 (Table A1.3). The decline in 1991 affected almost all fields, with the exception of chemical industry.[7] The situation has only worsened in the first half of 1992 (Table 7.1, Statistical Appendix). Probably some 40 to 50 percent of all enterprises are paralyzed for one reason or another. The primary reason for this performance is the chaos and disintegration of the Soviet Union and the contraction in economic activity and trade throughout the region in the last two years. The political turmoil in Georgia added to these difficult conditions.

Table A1.3
Changes in Industrial Output in 1991

Branch	Output Change, 1991/1990 (%)
Food Industry	82.2
Light industry	76.8
Machine building	82.5
Mining and metallurgy	57.2
Forest industries	70.2
Chemicals	98.6
Building materials	78.6
Industrial Sector	**79.3**

Source: Ministry of Industry

Reasons for Recent Performance

Curtailment of supplies of inputs. Imports of natural gas and fuel oil were cut during the blockade imposed on Georgia by the CIS after the unilateral declaration of independence in April 1991. Even raw materials such as cotton coming from other CIS Republics were embargoed. Examples are found everywhere. The manganese mine and the processing plant were completely stopped in winter because of lack of electricity; they are now operating at only 50 percent capacity because of lack of customers. They also lack wood to maintain underground galleries in the mine and are obliged to operate only the open pit mines. The fertilizer producing plant had to close some lines this winter due to the lack of gas. The situation is almost normal now, but the production in 1992 was probably half of 1991. As 80 percent of the raw materials needed by the light industry were imported (cotton, silk, wood, leather, etc.), the sector is similarly affected. In addition, rail transportation of other products was disrupted by the tensions in Ossetia and in Abkhazia.

Loss of market, particularly for military products. Due to the financial and economic crisis in the republics of the FSU, the demand for Georgian products has been sharply reduced. This has affected the military industry particularly badly. Thus, the Sukhoi plant (fighter planes) produces at 15 percent of its capacity. A general decline in investments in the region has led to reduced demand for equipment produced in Georgia. For example, the locomotive plant has only delivered seven locomotives to Ukraine by mid-1992, against 150-170 at the peak production time; and these locomotives have not even been paid for. Orders from Russia for locomotives are only a tenth of their previous order.

While these factors were the most proximate causes of the decline in industrial production, it may also have been adversely affected by the increased autonomy provided during this period to enterprise managers.[8] First, the severing of ties with the Union cut off a significant source of funds for the enterprise, which the Republican authorities could not compensate due to the tight fiscal constraints. Equally, enterprise managers were ill-prepared to take on the responsibilities of real managers: they do not have the necessary skills or experience to identify new markets for their products or inputs for their production. They also lack the basic tools which would enable them to take correct decisions: market information and contacts; management information systems; production controls, to name a few.

Enterprises have reacted to the crisis in several ways. These include: (i) diversification of production: for example, the enterprise producing fighter planes intends to produce civilian aircraft (mono and bi-motors) for local use; a garment plant has looked for subcontracts in Turkey, and is starting to assemble garment for a Turkish company; a shoe factory is now producing stylish models; (ii) lay-off of labor: most enterprises in difficulties have put their staff on unpaid leaves for two or three months; (iii) loans from the banks have also supported enterprises at the beginning, but banks now seem reluctant to lend to enterprises; (iv) arrears have been mounting; these arrears concern not only enterprises within Georgia, but they exist also between Georgian enterprises and enterprises in other FSU republics; and (v) use on a "borrowed basis" of raw materials from the strategic stockpiles deposited in the factory. Some enterprises have been authorized by the Ministry of Industry to use up to 30 percent of the stocks on this basis.

Constraints to Improved Performance

The thrust of industrial policy is to gradually integrate into the international economy. However, it also rightly emphasizes the need to restore close economic relations with the FSU in order to prevent a total economic collapse during the transition period. A prerequisite for formulating a strategy for integration in the international market is identifying the major constraints to improving the competitiveness of Georgian industry.

Inappropriate Industrial Structure

The existing industrial structure of Georgia was developed to serve the needs of an integrated Soviet economy, and was based on a complex system of direct and indirect taxes and subsidies. As Georgia integrates in the world economy and faces world prices for its inputs and outputs, the structure of industry is likely to change. As discussed in Chapter 1, Georgia has already suffered from a terms of trade shock as prices of imported energy have risen sharply. These prices are still below world prices and Georgian industry may expect a further deterioration in its terms of trade. The effect of this will be different for different parts of industry: those that are more intensive users of energy imports (such as machine building and chemicals) are likely to suffer most. With the exception of certain commodities (such as fertilizers and ferro-alloys), the quality of the Georgian manufactured products is also generally low by western standards. It is likely that several machine building and electronic enterprises in Georgia have a negative value added on the basis of international prices for inputs and outputs. These enterprises are simply wasting scarce capital and human resources.

Most of the equipment used by Georgian enterprises is Soviet made, and some is rather old. Although some enterprises have also been provided with western-made equipment (mostly the military complex, the chemical complex and some light industries), this equipment does not appear to be properly utilized due to low standards of quality control and maintenance, and inadequate incentives to improve efficiency.

Lack of Competition

Most enterprises are monopolistic or oligopolistic. Georgia lacks small, dynamic enterprises to provide domestic competition. Nor is there much competition from imports. Operating as monopolies in a shortage economy, practically on a cost-plus basis, enterprises had no incentive to upgrade quality or to reduce costs. Increasing competition will require facilitating the formation of new ventures, increased imports, the privatization and demonopolization of existing small and medium state enterprises, tight fiscal and financial policies, and effective threat of closure of unprofitable enterprises.

Managerial Capability and Corporate Governance

Enterprise managers are generally skilled and experienced in production techniques, but are lacking the skills or the experience needed to operate in competitive markets. They have very limited capabilities in marketing, finance, and other aspects of business management. While some may be able to acquire the new skills required, many of the present managers will have to be replaced. Moreover, cost accounting and management information systems are almost non existent.

Although the program of converting state-owned enterprises is under way, the corporate governance systems are still too rudimentary to provide managers and workers adequate incentives to improve productivity.

Inadequate Infrastructure and Services

Georgian enterprises are facing serious problems due to the extremely inadequate telecommunications services. The lack of a network of small workshops, capable of providing specialized services including sub-contracting, has forced enterprises to inefficiently seek self sufficiency and excessive vertical integration. The absence of large international trading companies also places Georgian enterprises at a distinct disadvantage in exploiting international trading opportunities. The underdeveloped banking system is another constraint. A particular deficiency is the difficulty of making prompt payments and obtaining even routine foreign exchange services, which are a prerequisite for integration in international markets. Nor are adequate consultant services available to assist enterprises in preparation and implementation of business plans and restructuring programs.

Despite these constraints, at least some parts of the industrial sector has the potential to become competitive provided an appropriate reform strategy is designed and implemented. This should exploit the advantages Georgia possesses, including a well educated and skilled work force; a reservoir of entrepreneurial talent that is engaged in the underground economy; low labor cost (in mid-1992 average wages in industry were Rbl 2100 per month); availability of plenty of equipment (though admittedly not all of good quality); and availability of raw material currently hoarded for "strategic" purposes.

Basic Industrial Strategy

The analysis above suggests some guidelines for formulating a pragmatic industrial strategy for Georgia. First, due to the very small domestic market, the industrial sector of Georgia should be encouraged to have a strong export orientation in an open economy. Second, Georgian industry must be encouraged to identify and shift to market niches, for example, "Cheap Good Quality Products"[9] or "specialty products".[10] Third, the government should resist the temptation to keep unprofitable activities afloat: rather it should encourage enterprises to restructure. And finally, the government should assist enterprises in the transition by facilitating trade with enterprises in other countries of the FSU, including by negotiating inter-state trade agreements; maintaining a stable payments system etc.

The transformation of the industrial sector will largely be done at the initiative of the enterprises in response to the progressive liberalization of the domestic economy and the freeing of international trade. However, the government has an important role to play in improving the policy framework and assisting enterprises through dissemination of training/retraining, setting up management standards and incentives, dissemination of market information, etc.. It should not interfere in the day-to-day management of the enterprises, nor attempt to pick winners.

The most important <u>role of the government</u> is to create a stable macroeconomic environment which would provide the right signals to the enterprises and ensure a level-playing field. It will also encourage foreign investment, which will bring in not only much needed investment, but also managerial skills.[11] The measures which need to be taken are discussed elsewhere in this report. To emphasize the most important:

(a)   Eliminate financial support to unprofitable state enterprises, unless it is provided in the context of a restructuring program. Enforce tax collection. Initiate the closure of some plants that are unambiguously unviable.

(b)   Accelerate the corporatization and privatization of state-owned enterprises, starting immediately with the privatization of the distribution system (shops, transport, warehouses (see Chapter 5).

(c)   Promote private sector development by improving the legal framework critical for its development (for example, the mining code, mortgage laws etc). In addition, institutions such as the arbitrage and judicial system to enable the resolution of commercial conflicts need to be established. Other measures to facilitate the growth of essential services (marketing consultants, accounting services etc) may also be required (see below). A review of the tax system to identify dis-incentives to the growth of new enterprises may also be useful.

(d)   Initiate the process of demonopolization by splitting up the associations and certain large enterprises (for example construction enterprises, wine enterprises) into smaller joint-stock companies, with the objective of introducing competition and facilitating privatization.   In addition, the preparation of a legal anti-monopoly framework is essential as well as the creation of an anti-monopoly agency to implement the law and monitor the issues of anti-competitive practices.

(e)   Stimulate restructuring through various measures.   For example, the government may encourage enterprises to restructure or privatize by giving them a part of the strategic stockpiles the government has accumulated.   Or it may provide financial assistance for a limited time to enterprises with viable restructuring plans.   Or grants may be provided to enterprises to create marketing units, or to enable them to finance feasibility studies for re-orienting their production to the Western markets.

(f)   Mobilize external technical assistance (preferably grants) to finance training of managers, in all aspects of business.

(g)   Mobilize external technical assistance (preferably grants) to finance entrepreneurship development in order to stimulate creation of new enterprises.   Disseminate information on HOW TO create and foster the development of enterprises.

(h)   Launch an emergency program to identify Georgian products which can be currently exported,[12] and support initial export efforts by promotion of Georgian goods (Georgian stand in major international exhibitions, organization of seminars, etc.).   Create an embryo of information office[13] enabling a foreign buyer to identify WHAT, WHERE and HOW to buy Georgian products and enterprises.

(i)   Facilitate the establishment of advisory services for enterprises, to be provided in the short term by external consulting firms, and subsequently also by domestic or joint venture advisory services.   The government's role is to mobilize technical assistance from external sources and to coordinate the use of such assistance in an efficient manner, as well as to promote the establishment of domestic advisory services.   A group of experts financed by grants could be assembled and be on call to assist enterprises in crisis to prepare and implement restructuring plans, or to wind-up.

(j)   Initiate and facilitate the introduction of improved accounting and auditing systems, in accordance with internationally accepted standards in order to provide boards of directors and managers of enterprises, as well as banks and foreign investors, with basic information to assess the financial performance of enterprises.   Extensive training of domestic accountants and auditors will be needed.

Last, but not the least, the government should review the functions of the various ministries, institutes and departments in the light of the disappearance of its role of owner and manager (the enterprises will be privatized over time).   Several ministries and organizations should be abolished and their remaining activity merged into ONE ministry of industry in charge of industrial policy, regulatory framework, standardization, and promotion activities.

Endnotes

1.   This annex is based on a more detailed description of the industrial sector.

2.   The rest comprised 258 "All Union" enterprises and 230 enterprises that were under joint Union-Republican ownership. The All Union enterprises were owned and controlled by about 35 Soviet industrial subsector ministries. These enterprises were given obligatory output targets which they were required to meet. They were provided with equipment and raw materials allocated by the central material resources ministry, and their investments were financed out of the Soviet State budget. The finished products were distributed according to the plan. These enterprises were mostly the larger enterprises in metallurgy, machine building and chemicals (but there were also 9 All-Union enterprises in the agrofood industry). Although the Republican authorities had some say over enterprises jointly owned between the Republic and the Union, to a large extent they were also controlled by the Moscow central authorities.

3.   The largest enterprises are concentrated in the mining and metallurgy, machine building and chemical subsectors. But it should be noted that even agrofood enterprises are large: only half of the enterprises have less than 100 employees while in Western Europe the corresponding share is close to 80 percent. The large size of the enterprises was only in part due to economies of scale and technical indivisibility. Factories in all subsectors--including light and agrofood industries--were often grouped into larger enterprises called "amalgamation", under a single management.

4.   Although figures are not available, an intelligent guess may be around 5 - 8 percent.

5.   For example, 70 percent of the one million micro-engines produced in Georgia were sent to Russia to produce washing machines. The tea-harvesters were built in Georgia on an Ukrainian chassis. 60 percent of the machines and electrotechnical products (engines, electric motors, transformers, lifts, cranes, etc.) were intended for Russian enterprises.

6.   But there are some underground private activities. It must be recalled that Georgia has a long tradition of parallel economy and it is difficult to identify the real ownership of a number of activities/workshops created within the framework of State enterprises. A relatively large number of small semi-private workshops seem to exist that produce mainly products not currently produced by the State enterprises (fancier consumer products, products in shortages, etc.), using facilities and/or raw materials from the State enterprise.

7.   This is probably due to a priority allocation of gas in a period of shortage due to the strategic impact of fertilizers for agriculture and its large exports outside the ruble zone.

8.   New legislation gives enterprise managers considerable autonomy in current management, including freedom to set output prices of most products in the domestic market, to lay off excess workers, and after they have fulfilled the remaining state orders, to sell their products domestically or export them.

9.   For example, Georgia might develop a garment industry, as did Turkey in the 1980s. In addition to the huge ex-Soviet market, it might export to the West, but this would require the negotiation of quotas with major importers such as the EC and USA.

10.   For example, Georgia might be a good location for the production of essential oils and aroma for perfume, cosmetic and food industry. It might also be a location to produce certain extracts for pharmaceutical industry. Georgia might also develop a packaging industry, glass and plastic bottles, cartons, wood and plastic crates to improve the image and the shelf life of its food products.

11.   As experience elsewhere has shown, foreign investment is attracted more by a stable macroeconomic environment, rather than by selective tax preferences for foreign investors.

12.   Given the price distortions which will prevail for some time, some products which can be exported today may have no medium term future in export markets. However, their current export will (a) bring much needed foreign exchange, (b) improve the information base and the skills of Georgian managers, and (c) soften the transition impact.

13.   Given the lack of experience in these matters of the current staff of the ministries and government institutions, it would be advisable to staff such an office with young external recruitees who speak foreign languages, may be with the support of one expatriate for a limited period.

ANNEX 2

The Energy Sector[1]

Introduction

Georgia was a net energy importing republic in the FSU. Since independence, it has experienced very large increases in the cost of energy imports. Georgia has also found it difficult to secure energy supplies due in part to its political differences with other members of the CIS, as well as shortages of electricity in the Caucasus brought about by the closure of Armenia's nuclear power station in 1988. Shortages of energy have contributed to the shut down of a large part of industry and is likely to cause hardship for the population during the winter. Adjusting to these new realities will be the important challenge for the sector in the coming months and years.

Recent Developments in Energy Consumption and Availability

A summary energy balance for Georgia for the 1975-90 period is shown below. Data for 1991 and 1992 are not currently available in a similar form.

Table A2.1 Energy Balance, 1975-90 (millions tons of coal equivalent)				
	1975	**1980**	**1985**	**1990**
Total Resources	27791	23322	23975	22323
- Domestic fuels	1490	5926	1611	820
- Hydropower	871	2102	2035	2470
- Imports	23987	14544	19093	17949
- Other resources	13	29	75	30
- Opening inventory	1430	721	1161	1054
Total uses	27791	23322	23975	22323
- Domestic use of which:	17639	16079	18901	19160
-- Use in energy sector	6730	8385	9578	11011
-- Use in industry, etc	10909	7694	9323	8149
-- Exports	9104	6406	3915	2323
-- Closing inventory	1048	837	1159	840

Source: Commission of Statistics

The table captures the major features of the energy situation in Georgia, which can be summarized as follows:

(a)   Energy consumption is very high. In 1990, consumption of energy was approximately 2,450 kilograms of oil-equivalent (koe) per person, about 40 percent of the level in Russia (5,990 koe per person). However, with a per capita GNP approximately half that of Russia, Georgia's energy consumption per unit of GNP is only 20 percent less than in Russia, the most energy intensive economy of the FSU. Similarly, electricity consumption per unit of GNP in Georgia was 90 percent of Russian levels in 1990.

(b)   Industry is the major user of energy, consuming more than half of electricity and heat, more than three-quarters of fuel oil, and almost half of gas; the transport sector consumes almost all the diesel and gasoline, and households consume half the gas and about one quarter of electricity and heat. Oil accounted for 44 percent of primary energy consumption in 1990, gas for 29.3 percent, hydropower for 17.5 percent and coal for 7.3 percent.

(c)   Over the past decade, Georgia's energy resources and production capacity have been depleting, and the rate of depletion has accelerated in the past two years. Despite investments in exploration and field development, crude oil output has fallen by 95 percent from its peak of 3.5 million tons in 1983 to 150,000 tons in 1991, and coal and lignite output has fallen by 57 percent since its peak production in the early 1970s. This decline was largely due to the decision to substitute cheap gas from other republics for coal and lignite in the power system. In electricity, production has stagnated (with the exception of 1989) during the past five years, reflecting the effect of climate on hydropower output and the absence of investments in new plants.

(d)   Within the FSU, Georgia was a net energy importer, on both an annual and seasonal basis;[2] in 1990, imports of energy amounted to approximately 80 percent of total available energy resources, and energy exports compensated for only 13 percent of imports. Dependence on imports increased gradually during the past decade, reflecting reduced domestic production of crude oil and coal. Energy exports declined both absolutely and as a share of energy imports.[3]

(e)   The most important energy imports, measured in standard energy units, were, natural gas, fuel oil, crude oil, electricity and gasoline. Out of total imports of 17,949 tons of coal equivalent (tce) in 1990, imports of natural gas amounted to 35 percent, fuel oil 21 percent, crude oil 17 percent, electricity 8 percent and gasoline 6 percent.

(f)   All of domestic consumption of gas is imported; so is most of crude oil consumption,[4] more than half of the consumption of fuel oil, and more than a third of electricity consumption.

(g)   The most important source of imports is Russia; until 1991, virtually all crude oil and oil products came from Russia, as did all natural gas and more than half of the electricity (the remainder coming from Azerbaijan). While Russian supplies of oil and oil products and electricity remain important, since the beginning of 1992 natural gas is primarily imported from Turkmenistan.

(h)   Georgia's own reserves of coal and oil, although not insubstantial in physical terms, are inferior to resources elsewhere in the FSU and therefore have not been developed extensively. In 1990, Georgia's energy production was 10.4 percent lower than in 1985. Domestic production of oil increased in the early 1970s and reached 3.5 million tons in 1984, but has declined since then as existing fields depleted and investments in exploration did not bear fruit. Similarly, coal production totalled 2.5 million tons a decade ago, but has fallen to less than one million tons in 1991 as low prices of other energy products encouraged conversion of coal-fired thermal power stations in recent years, and industrial stagnation in the past decade discouraged production. Georgia's most important and most developed energy resource has been hydropower generation, which produces 7 billion kwh annually; thermal power stations fuelled by imported fuel oil or gas provide another 6 billion kwh each year.

(i)   In 1991-92, the prices of imported energy have increased dramatically (para. 6); between December 1991 and June 1992, the import price of gas has risen from Rbl 51 per '000 cubic meters to Rbl 1,710; that of crude oil has risen from Rbl 90 per ton to Rbl 1,000; and that of imported electricity has risen from 5 kopeks per kwh to Rbl 1.93 in the case of purchases from Russia and Rbl 4.72 in the case of purchases from Azerbaijan. Despite these price increases, international prices are still considerably higher, and further increases will soon be forthcoming. Already energy related subsidies are considerable (see Chapter 1).

Major Issues and Challenges

The collapse of the Soviet Union and Georgia's independence has led to radical changes in the energy sector. First, as mentioned earlier, Georgia has to pay much higher prices for importing its energy requirements. The cost of energy imports is likely to rise even more in the near future. How best to reduce wasteful use of energy has become a major issue. Second, obtaining imports of energy from traditional suppliers (e.g., Russia) is getting increasingly difficult, partly because of political differences, but also because of the shortage of electricity in the Caucasus because of the closure of the nuclear power plant in Armenia. The need to re-establish supply relationships with the newly independent countries of the FSU, as well as diversify sources of supply have become urgent concerns. Finally, the collapse of central control and management of energy supply and demand in Georgia requires that Georgia develop its own capacities for planning and management of energy production and use.

The government has responded to these new circumstances in a variety of ways. First, domestic energy prices were raised, although in most cases these prices still do not reflect fully the cost to the economy of energy imports. In particular, prices of gas, electricity and heat for households have remained unchanged to date, partly subsidized through the budget (heating) and partly by industrial users (electricity). Second, through the Ministry of Energy the government is negotiating the purchase of energy imports from the newly independent countries of the FSU as well as other sources. Gas supplies have been negotiated from Turkmenistan and Iran: Turkmenistan was expected to supply 5.2 billion cubic meters in 1992 and 1993, while Iran was to supply 400 million cubic meters in 1992 and 2 billion cubic meters in 1993. Oil and petroleum product supplies have been negotiated with Russia and Azerbaijan, which have also been the major suppliers of electricity. All these contracts have been negotiated at much higher prices than in the past, though these are still below international prices. The government has also indicated that it intends to accelerate development of indigenous energy resources in order to reduce reliance on imported energy in the longer term. In addition to solar and wind power, and small and micro hydropower schemes, interest in which is motivated in part by environmental concerns, expansion of coal and lignite mining for thermal power production is now being promoted, and initial discussions have been started with foreign investors concerning joint ventures in oil exploration and exploitation. Finally, the Ministry of Energy has consolidated all aspects of energy in Georgia; this is the first step in the long term process of reforming and restructuring energy sector organization and management.

(i) Energy Pricing

The recent increases in imported energy prices has increased the sensitiveness of the authorities to the efficient use of energy.[5] This combined with the difficult budgetary situation led the government to increase domestic prices of energy substantially (Table A2.2). In early 1992, the domestic wholesale price of crude oil was raised from Rbl 90 per ton to Rbl 1,000, and the domestic price of imported crude has subsequently been raised to between Rbl 4,000-9,000 per ton; ex-refinery prices of petroleum products have in principle been set at international levels, and private sector trade in these products has been allowed. At the same time, the domestic price of imported natural gas was raised from Rbl 51 per '000 cubic meters to Rbl 1710.

These price increases should result in reducing wasteful energy consumption, provided users are not compensated directly or indirectly for the higher prices.[6] The increase in energy prices will also stimulate investments in energy development: in hydropower for electricity, in coal, and in secondary and tertiary recovery of oil. Over time, the elimination of wasteful consumption, and increased production of energy should reduce dependency on imports.

In spite of the recent changes in the pricing regime for energy products, there is as yet no overall framework or strategy for energy pricing. Energy pricing is a bizarre and complex mix of world price principles, CIS negotiated import prices, domestic cost-plus pricing practices, free market and regulated prices, and subsidies and cross-subsidization.[7]

The existence of this mixed pricing system is in part because pricing decisions have been made largely in response to particular events, mainly increases in import costs, which have been sporadic and specific to individual fuels. In part it is also because the government has found it politically difficult either to pass on to end-users the increased costs or to allow prices to be determined in the market. As a result, there are large differences between costs and prices of energy products, which require direct subsidies from the budget or indirect subsidization from some users.

The government needs to urgently define and announce a pricing policy for energy. This is important, first, because otherwise the burden of subsidizing energy would become too heavy and threaten the integrity of the budget. Continuing energy subsidies would also discourage efficient use and encourage investment in industries and activities that are not competitive at international prices. Given the difficult economic environment, there is no scope for these mistakes. It is therefore essential that the government announce a policy of eliminating energy subsidies over a short period. Second, price increases for energy need to establish appropriate relative price relationships between different energy sources, particularly those where substitution is possible; increases in the price of heat for households, for example, will result in switching of energy consumption to electricity if the latter's price is not also adjusted.

		Price (rubles)			
Product	Unit	1989	1990	1991	1992[c]
Crude Oil					
-domestic	ton	78	82	1000	4000
-import	ton			4-9000	
Fuel Oil					
-import	ton				13000
-industry	ton	27	27		13000
Natural Gas					
-import	'000 m3	15.5	42	51	1710
-household	'000 m3	50	50	50	50[b]
-industry	'000 m3	30	52	61	1000[b]
Electricity					
-industry	kwh				2.47
-state orgs.	kwh				0.56
-households	kwh				0.12
-import	kwh				1.93[a]

Table A2.2
Evolution of Energy Prices, 1989-92

[a] Imports from Russia; imports from Azerbaijan are Rbl 4.72 per kwh, from Turkey USc1.6 (Rbl 2.1) per kwh.

[b] Proposals for increasing household and industry prices to Rbl 500 and 3000 per '000 m3 are being discussed.

[c] As of mid-1992

Source: Ministry of Energy and Bureau of Statistics

(ii) Energy Institutions and Organization

As discussed in the report, the liberalization of energy prices, and appropriate setting of administered prices, are necessary for bringing about more efficient energy consumption and supply. However, these reforms are not sufficient: there is also need for institutional reforms that will make users and producers more sensitive to prices. These include clarification of ownership rights in the energy sector, establishment of the appropriate role of the state in regulating and managing the energy sector and the transition to a more market-oriented industry, and establishment of efficient agencies, enterprises and utilities for operating energy operations. Although the movement towards a market economy opens up substantial opportunities for private sector involvement, particularly in the petroleum industry, the government will continue to play a significant role in the energy sector, not only as framer of the policy environment but also as owner of energy assets, particularly gas and electricity networks.

The focal point within the government for the energy sector is the Ministry of Energy. The major energy subsectors remain as departments under the Ministry of Energy; these include electricity (Gruzglavenergo), oil (Gruzneft), gas (Gruzgaz), and coal and lignite (Gruzugol), all of whom rely significantly upon the central government budget for their financing. The Ministry has the responsibility not only for planning, coordination, regulation and strategy but also has considerable day-to-day responsibility for all energy operations. The major priority for the government over the past year was to bring energy issues under its management and control. At the same time, the process of "corporatizing" the energy sector and removing it from the Ministry's management has begun in an informal way through the creation of "companies". However, these organizations have no legal form and are dependent on a consensus that their organizational and management form should be independent of government. They still remain very dependent upon the state for their funding.

The appropriate form of organization of the energy sector for the future is a major issue with several dimensions. First, a reorganization of energy branches should be carried out: the initial step should be to create energy companies with separate legal personas, which would permit them to be privatized or managed as commercially oriented enterprises under state ownership. One issue faced by the corporatized energy entities will be their form of internal organization. Currently, Gruzglavenergo, Gruzugol, Gruzneft, Gruzgaz and Gruztransgaz are groupings of government departments and divisions organized along traditional ministry lines. Work will be required to reconfigure each organization to enable it to carry out its technical functions and to operate along commercial lines. This is of particular importance in the oil sector because of the need to establish an effective institutional presence to negotiate Georgian participation in the proposed Baku-Poti oil pipeline.

Second, initial decisions should be taken as to which activities are to remain within the state sector and which are to be privatized or opened to private sector initiative. There appears to be considerable interest in encouraging private sector involvement in various parts of the energy sector: for example, Gruzglavenergo has indicated that it would be interested in leasing or selling some of the small hydropower stations. However, experience from other countries suggests that privatization and private sector involvement in this area is difficult to bring about, and it may be more realistic for Gruzglavenergo to put its efforts chiefly into the process of creating an efficient and reliable public utility capable of delivering a good service. This is not to say that government or Gruzglavenergo should refuse to negotiate arrangements for private sector involvement if such offers materialize: merely to caution that private sector interest is only likely to develop once a record of good management and operation of the generation, transmission and distribution system has been established.

The prospects for private sector involvement are better in other energy branches; for example, efforts have already begun to encourage private and foreign involvement in the oil industry, both in exploration and exploitation and also in petroleum product marketing. The major priority for government action in exploration and exploitation is to establish the basic legal framework for use of natural resources. Currently, Georgia has no legislative basis for oil exploration and exploitation, and work needs to begin in this area as soon as possible if foreign investment and private sector involvement is to be secured.

Third, in connection with establishing a legal and regulatory basic framework, the appropriate role for the state must be clarified, including the relationship between the Ministry and the state enterprises in the sector. One issue that requires special attention is the separation of regulatory and operational responsibilities. In several other countries, the government has created national oil and gas corporations whose primary responsibility is to manage production of reserves under their control. However, the government has often given these corporations some of the regulatory and ownership functions that should remain with the state; for example, the corporation may be given the power to determine the disposition of concessions to foreign investors and thereby to operate in effect a continued monopoly. Such arrangements should be avoided, and a careful delineation of the respective roles of government agencies and state enterprises should be ensured.

(iii) Energy Demand and Supply

Decisions about energy investment and future energy production must be based on an assessment of projected trends in energy demand. This is particularly difficult in present circumstances given the major disruptions that have occurred recently (which make past patterns an unreliable guide to the future), and the likely transformation of production and consumption patterns that will occur as the economy is liberalized. Broadly speaking however, it is likely that the demand for energy will be considerably reduced in the foreseeable future. This is not only because increase in prices will encourage more efficient use of energy and a less energy intensive pattern of production, but also because the economy will not be growing at least for the next few years.

While it is difficult, forecasting of energy demand is very important to determine the level and structure of those investments that state enterprises will be required to make. These investments tend to be large and mistakes based on optimistic forecasts can be very costly. Thus, it is recommended that the Ministry of Energy and Ministry of Economy should begin work to create a perspective of energy demand as a basis for future planning and assessment of investment proposals. Such work will require close cooperation with the statistical agencies.

In order to reduce dependence on imported energy, the government issued a decree in mid-1992 promoting accelerated development of domestic coal and lignite mining and construction of coal and lignite-fired thermal power stations. It also committed to financing investigations into geothermal, wind and solar energy. While the government's reaction to the energy shortages and price increases of imported energy is understandable, Georgia should be cautious about undertaking large investments in energy production until their economic viability has been assessed. The evaluation of energy supply options should take into account the growth of aggregate demand for energy, including prospects for export, and whether increased efficiency in energy use is offset or not by increased demand produced by the growth of new economic activities. In addition, proposed investments should be evaluated on the basis of the relative efficiency of importing energy or producing domestically. Indeed, while the political and economic disruptions of the last few years understandably lead the government to consider ways of insulating the domestic economy from further shocks, Georgia's energy position, and in particular its strong seasonal dimension, suggests that the country has much to gain from preserving trade opportunities in energy.

However, the most urgent assessments are required for the major energy resources. Probable reserves of oil are currently estimated to be 300 million tons, and potential for further finds is considered good. Geological survey for oil has been conducted all over Georgia, but not in a very intensive fashion. Proven coal and lignite reserves amount to approximately 450 million tons, and probable reserves a further 700 million tons.

In the case of oil, there is a need to reassess existing geological information to determine the prospects for further crude oil discoveries and the commercial viability of existing reserves, and to determine how new investments by competent investors can be promoted. Moreover, the economics of the refinery at Batumi need to be established, as a basis for determining the viability of continuing operations and the economic viability of rehabilitation or replacement projects. In the case of coal and lignite, costs of mining need to be calculated to determine the feasibility of export and the viability of electricity production based on coal and lignite.

Evaluation of coal and lignite mining needs to be conducted within the broader context of a least-cost development analysis of the power sector. Such an analysis is required to rank the options--hydropower plants of various sizes and thermal plants fired by coal, lignite, oil or gas, etc--available for the development of electricity and power. Such an analysis would also provide the basis for establishing the long-run marginal cost of electricity, which in turn would be the basis for establishing a rational structure of electricity tariffs for different groups of consumers. It should be emphasized, however, that increases in electricity prices should not be delayed until this analysis, which will take some time to complete, is finished.

Endnotes

1. This annex is based on a more detailed description of the energy sector, which may be obtained upon request.

2. Import dependency has a strong seasonal dimension in Georgia, because of seasonal differences in hydropower plants' capacity to supply; production is highest in summer, when it appears that Georgia is just about self-sufficient or even a net exporter of electricity, but demand is highest in winter, when shortfalls between domestic production and electricity demand are met from imported electricity.

3. According to official statistics, the domestic energy supply deteriorated in Georgia throughout the 1980s, when there was a rapid decline in the output of the "fuel-energy complex" and the "fuel industry". According to these statistics, the fuel industry had a production index of 66 in 1985 and 32 in 1990 (with 1980=100), reflecting lower coal and oil production, and since electricity output remained more or less stable throughout the period, the index of the "fuel-energy complex" (which is the synthetic indicator for fuel and electricity) fell from 79 in 1985 to 59 in 1990.

4. In 1991, domestic crude oil production, which was sold into Georgia's only refinery at Batumi, met only 5 percent or so of petroleum product requirements.

5. The large increase in imported energy prices have been mainly responsible for the adverse terms of trade shock suffered by Georgia during 1991-92. It is difficult to give a precise indication of the size of the terms of trade effect because it has not been possible to obtain volume and price data for all traded products; however, the scale is almost certainly very large, in view of the fact that, in 1991, energy imports were a little less than 10 percent of total imports, and energy import prices have risen by 50-100 times already in the first half of 1992. Further terms of trade deterioration may be expected as imported energy prices are raised to international levels in the next year or so.

6. While hard data on energy inefficiency and waste is hard to come by, there is significant scope for energy saving. For example, the Ministry of Economy considers that several major energy-intensive industries, such as the ferro-processing complex, would be uneconomic at world prices for energy; the lack of meters in households to measure and charge for gas use results in extensive waste, especially when alternative sources of power and heat are not available; and large amounts of fuel are being used inefficiently in district heating schemes because of poor insulation of pipes and residences.

7. The case of oil and petroleum products illustrates this state of affairs. Domestic crude is sold by Gruzneft, the department for oil in the Ministry of Energy, to Batumi refinery. While officially Gruzneft is free to price its oil at whatever price it wishes, it charges only Rbl 4,000 per ton ($ 27 at the exchange rate of Rbl 150/$), or about 30 percent of the world price for low-sulfur crude. This it does "because it has the national interest at heart". The refinery is also supplied by Gruzneftproduct, the petroleum product distribution department. The source of this oil is crude oil imported from Russia at contract prices varying in early 1992 between 4,000 and 9,000 ($ 27 and 60 per ton); these negotiated prices are approximately 30 - 65 percent of the world price. Batumi refinery is authorized to sell its products to Gruzneftproduct at ex-refinery prices equal to world prices, which it currently does, but Gruzneftproduct forms its retail prices on a cost-plus basis by adding a margin, authorized by government, to cover its distribution costs and by adding a 28% sales tax which is remitted to government. The current price for fuel oil sold to industry is Rbl 13,000 per ton, which is 15 percent below the world price; for gasoline, the official retail price for sale to the population is Rbl 8-10 ($ 0.05-0.07) per liter, while private traders, some of whom are now importing small quantities, have been selling gasoline for Rbl 22 ($ 0.15) per liter.

BIBLIOGRAPHY

Committee on Social and Economic Information, Georgia (1992): Report on Social Economic Conditions, Jan-May 1992.

Dornbusch and Fisher (1986): Stopping Inflation Past and Present, Paper presented at Seminar on Adjustment Policies and External Finance, Washington, D.C., June 1986.

Dornbusch, Starzeger and Wolf (1990): Extreme Inflation: Dynamics and Stabilization

Grossman, G. (1977): The 'Second Economy' of the USSR, in Problems of Communism, 26.

Kochav and Sood (1992): Enterprise Reform in Central and Eastern Europe (draft mimeo).

IMF (June 1992): Monetary Policy in the Ruble Area, (mimeo).

IMF (June 1992): Review of Experience with Programs in Eastern Europe.

IMF (August 1992): Georgia: Basic Issues in Taxation, Budgetary and Social Expenditures Policy for an Economy in Transition.

IMF (August 1992): Georgia: A Short Term Action Program for the Reform of the Banking System.

Milanovic, B. (1992): Distributional Incidence of Cash and In-Kind Transfers in Eastern Europe and Russia, World Bank (mimeo).

Suny, R. (1988): The Making of the Georgian Nation, Indiana University Press.

Tarr, David (1992): Terms of Trade Effects on Countries of the Former Soviet Union, World Bank (mimeo).

Van Wijnbergen, Sweder (1992): Economic Aspects of Enterprise Reform in Eastern Europe, World Bank (mimeo).

World Bank (1992): Russian Economic Reform: Crossing the Threshhold of Structural Change (CEM).

Statistical Appendix

STATISTICAL APPENDIX - CONTENTS

Table 1.1 – Georgia: Social Indicators of Republics of Former Soviet Union

	People per km sq	Housing m2 per head 1990	Doctors per 10000 persons 1989	Hospital beds per 10000 1990	Life Expectancy in years 1990
Georgia	78.4	18.8	59.2	110.7	72.1
Russia	8.7	16.4	46.9	137.5	69.3
Ukraine	86.0	17.8	44.0	135.5	70.5
Belarus	49.4	17.9	40.5	132.3	71.3
Uzbekistan	46.3	12.1	35.8	123.7	69.5
Kazakhstan	6.2	14.2	41.2	136.2	68.8
Azerbaijan	82.4	12.5	39.3	102.2	71.0
Armenia	113.3	15.0	42.8	89.8	71.8
Lithuania	57.2	...	46.1	124.4	71.5
Moldova	129.6	17.9	40.0	131.4	68.7
Latvia	41.6	19.8	49.6	148.1	69.6
Kyrgyzstan	22.3	12.1	36.7	119.8	68.8
Tadjikistan	37.4	9.3	27.1	105.8	69.6
Estonia	35.1	21.6	45.7	121.0	70.0

Source: Statistical Handbook, GOSKOMSTAT–USSR, 1990

Table 1.2 – Georgia: Social Indicators for Georgia and Countries at Similar Level of Income

	GDP per capita (dollars)	Infant Mortality (per 1000 births)	Life Expectancy (years)	Primary School Enrollment (%)	Illiteracy (%)
Romania	1640	23	69.6	95	0
Poland	1690	16	71.3	99	0
Europe	1665	20	70.5	97	0
Jordan	1730	51	67.3	....	20
Turkey	1640	60	66.6	100	19
Tunisia	1440	44	66.7	100	35
Middle East	1600	52	66.9	100	25
Jamaica	1500	16	73.2	100	....
Peru	1160	69	62.7	100	15
Colombia	1260	37	68.8	100	13
Panama	1840	21	72.6	100	12
Chile	1940	17	72	100	7
Americas	1540	32	69.9	100	12
Georgia 1\	1250	20	72.1	100	0

1\ Data for Georgia 1991–92, other countries, 1989–91

Source: Social Indicators of Development 1991–92, World Bank, 1992.

Table 1.3 – Georgia: Population and Employment – Summary Table
(Thousands)

	1987	1988	1989	1990	1991
Total Population	5356	5396	5414	5422	5420
Males	2538	2561	2571	2579	..
Females	2819	2838	2843	2343	..
Urban	2930	2989	3014	3029	3024
Rural	2426	2409	2400	2393	2397
Below Working Ages	1423	1423	1421	1417	..
Working–Age Population	3024	3042	3036	3027	..
Above Working Ages	910	934	957	278	..
Total Employed Population	2647	2650	2624	2685	2543
State Sector	2199	2205	2148	2087	1886
Collective Farms	264	249	218	200	154
Cooperatives	5	19	48	137	109
Individual Labor Activities	4	6	5	4	4
Private Subsidiary Agriculture	176	171	206	225	352
Private Agriculture	..	..	..	31	36

Source: Committee for Social & Economic Information, Feb 1993

Table 1.4 – Georgia: Labor Force Participation Rate (1989 Census)

	Total	0–15	16–19	20–24	25–29	30–34	35–39	40–44	45–49	50–54	55–59	60–64	over 65
Total Population (thous.	5401	1423	335	414	467	416	362	261	296	345	304	298	478
Employed (thous.)	2634	2	118	275	320	356	319	231	258	285	201	128	80
Labor Force Part. (%)	49	0	35	66	68	86	88	89	87	83	66	43	17
Males:													
Population (thous.)	2562	725	175	203	226	201	175	125	139	164	141	130	158
Employed (thous.)	1414	1	64	151	209	193	168	119	130	149	120	72	41
Labor Force Part. (%)	55	0	36	74	92	96	96	95	94	91	85	55	26
Females:													
Population (thous.)	2839	698	160	210	241	215	187	136	157	181	163	167	319
Employed (thous.)	1221	1	54	124	169	164	153	112	128	137	83	57	38
Labor Force Part. (%)	43	0	34	59	70	76	82	83	82	76	51	34	12

Source: Committee for Social & Economic Information, Feb 1993

Table 2.1 – Georgia: Net Material Product and Gross Domestic Product
(Mln of Rubles, at Current Prices)

	1980	1987	1988	1989	1990	1991	1992 1/
Net material product 2/	8,052	9,690	9,900	9,989	10,866	14,737	82,755
Salaries	2,697	3,761	4,075	4,153	5,128	9,593	41,526
Social security pay.	167	317	290	356	420	1,399	12,458
Profits	1,353	1,397	1,493	2,016	1,884	1,850	8,058
Other	3,835	4,214	4,042	3,465	3,433	1,896	20,713
Non-material sphere:							
Value-added	949	2,594	2,567	2,239	1,875	3,809	36,794
inc. Housing rents	83	91	93	89	90	169	828
Net material product	9,001	12,284	12,466	12,229	12,740	18,545	119,550
Depreciation in both spheres	1,181	1,933	2,040	2,127	2,175	2,221	14,847
Gross domestic product	10,181	14,217	14,506	14,355	14,915	20,766	134,397

1/ Official estimates of economic activity in 1992 do not account for the Abkhazia region.
The adjusted figures provided below account for this omission and are based on
the IMF's estimates of the share of NMP for the Abkhazia region.
2/ Net of losses of material stocks.
Source: Committee for Social and Economic Information, Feb 1993., IMF.

Table 2.2 – Georgia: Net Material Product in Current Prices
(Mln Rubles)

	1988	1989	1990	1991	1992 \1
Net Material Product	9898	9989	10866	14737	82755
By Origin:					
Agriculture/livestock	3074	2830	4046	4920	24347
Industry	4032	4009	3800	6148	28201
Construction	1319	1383	1194	1318	6453
Transport/communication	399	428	532	553	16969
Trade/catering	455	520	613	819	1909
Other branches	621	820	681	980	4876
By Final Use:					
Total Consumption	7655	7982	9456	12866	69587
Individual consumption	6650	6909	8263	11028	61472
Consumption by					
service institutions	776	808	846	1242	5222
Consumption by					
science institutions	229	265	347	596	2892
Total Accumulation	2359	1710	1748	1623	−879
Net fixed investments	1360	969	589	−92	−1355
Stock changes	999	741	1159	1715	476
Losses on fixed capital	141	182	136	336	20280
Trade Balance	−256	−116	−474	−89	−6232
Exports	5901	6084	5983	5338	18081
Imports	6157	5968	6457	5427	24313

(continued)

Table 2.2 (cont'd) – Georgia: Net Material Product in Current Prices
(Percentage of NMP)

	1988	1989	1990	1991	1992\1
By Origin:					
Agriculture/livestock	31	28	37	33	29
Industry	41	40	35	42	34
Construction	13	14	11	9	8
Transport/communication	4	4	5	4	21
Trade/catering	5	5	6	6	2
Other branches	6	8	6	7	6
By Final Use:					
Total Consumption	77	80	87	87	84
Individual consumption	67	69	76	75	74
Consumption by service institutions	8	8	8	8	6
Consumption by science institutions	2	3	3	4	3
Total Accumulation	24	17	16	11	−1
Net fixed investments	14	10	5	−1	−2
Stock changes	10	7	11	12	1
Losses on fixed capital	1	2	1	2	25
Trade Balance	3	−1	4	−1	−8
Exports	60	61	55	36	22
Imports	62	60	59	37	29

\1 Official estimates of economic activity in 1992 do not account for the Abkhazia region. The adjusted figures provided below account for this omission and are based on the IMF's estimates of theshare of NMP in the Abkhazia region.

Source: Committee for Social & Economic Information. Feb 1993., IMF.

Table 2.3 – Georgia: Growth of Net Material Product at Constant 1990 Prices
(Annual Percent Change)

	1988	1989	1990	1991	1992
Net Material Product	5.8	−4.8	−12.4	−20.6	−45.6
Agriculture and livestock	7.1	−24.3	61.8	−10.6	−48.8
Industry	5.8	−6.9	−29.9	−24.4	−33.9
Construction	8.0	2.3	−33.9	−35.9	−50.0
Transport and Communication	27.4	2.1	−5.8	−34.0	−64.9
Trade and catering	11.0	0.9	−18.1	−15.5	−79.0
Other material branches	−14.6	61.0	−49.9	−25.3	−34.8

Source: Ministry of Economy

Table 3.1 - Georgia: Total Exports and Imports of Georgia 1988-92

	(million rubles)			(as % of GDP)	
	Ruble Area	Other	Total	Ruble Area	Other
EXPORTS					
1988	5508	393	5901	38.0	2.7
1989	5719	365	6084	40.0	2.5
1990	5724	251	5975	38.0	1.7
1991	5287	51	5338	23.0	0.2
1992	14660	1628	16289	11.0	1.2
IMPORTS					
1988	5218	1275	6493	36.0	8.3
1989	4888	1581	6469	34.0	11.0
1990	4948	1891	6839	33.0	12.7
1991	4542	832	5374	19.4	3.5
1992	18513	3391	21904	13.8	2.5
NET BALANCE					
1988	290	-882	-592		
1989	831	-1216	-385		
1990	776	-1640	-864		
1991	745	-781	-36		
1992	-3853	-1763	-5616		

Source: Committee for Social and Economic Information, Feb 1993

Table 3.2 – Georgia: Total Trade by Commodity Groups in 1991–92
(Million Rubles)

COMMODITY GROUPS	EXPORTS		IMPORTS	
	1991	1992 /1	1991	1992 /1
Energy	44.3	...	595.6	736.0
Oil & Natural gas	0.4	...	338.1	6,769.0
All other types of energy	3.7	56.9	8.4	193.3
Ferrous Metallurgy	...	...	11.3	400.3
Metallurgy	308.5	5,680.5	432.7	554.4
Chemical & Oil Products	60.5	3,256.1	86.4	644.9
Metal Construction	342.9	541.9	522.5	890.1
Wood Industry	1,487.6	1,541.8	809.9	1,121.6
Construction	80.2	430.1	249.3	564.6
Light Industry	27.9	28.8	142.9	805.7
Food Industry	1,195.5	1,510.4	1,040.1	3,167.9
Other Industry	1,145.5	2,663.4	750.4	2,439.3
Agriculture	126.5	526.8	198.0	1,388.9
Other Material Industry	514.5	52.3	241.4	2,228.0
Total	5,338.0	16,289.0	5,427.0	21,904.0

\1 Estimates for 1992 are based on data for the first nine months.

Source: Committee for Social & Economic Information, Feb 1993

Table 3.3 – Georgia: Imports of Energy and Fuel in 1992 \1
(Thousand Tonnes, Unless Otherwise Indicated)

FUEL & ENERGY	TOTAL	Russia	Azerbaijan	Turkmenistan	Average Price Ruble/tonne
Coal	2	2	...	...	510
Natural gas (mn. m3)	6769	...	...	6769	4214
Liquid Gas	261	248	13	...	9400
Heating Oil	305	305	...	...	6500
Diesel Fuel	99	50	49	...	16000
Motor Fuel	64	60	3	...	31000
Kerosene	5	5	...	...	7500

\1 Estimates for 1992 are based on the first 9 months.

Source: Committee for Social & Economic Information, Feb 1993

Table 3.4 – Georgia: Calculations of Parity between the Ruble and Dollar for Grocery Items

	1990			1992 /1		
	Price (1kg)		Relative	Price (1kg)		Relative
	Rubles	US $	Price (PPP)	Rubles	US $	Price (PPP)
Bread			.40			3.50
–Wheat	.4	1.10	.35	6.50	1.25	5.20
–Rye bread	.22	.75	.30	1.70	.85	2.00
–Rice	.80	1.10	.73	17.50	1.20	14.25
Meat			1.05			15.00
–Beef	4.0	4.0	1.00	75.0	4.40	17.00
–Pork	4.0	3.65	1.10	70.0	4.15	14.00
–Mutton	4.0	4.25	.95	65.0	4.70	14.00
–Poultry	2.40	2.00	1.20	35.0	2.25	15.00
Fish	1.40	5.60	.25	37.0	6.15	6.00
–Seafood	1.40	5.60	.25	37.0	6.15	6.00
Milk, and dairy			.55			10.00
–Milk	.40	0.75	.53	4.0	.85	5.90
–Cheese	3.20	7.25	.45	160.0	7.80	20.50
–Eggs (10)	.90	1.20	.75	35.0	2.15	15.50
Oil			.85			16.00
–Butter	3.60	4.35	.85	87.0	4.75	18.30
–Vegetable Oil	1.60	1.80	.90	22.50	2.25	10.00
–Margarine	1.60	1.90	.85	35.0	2.15	15.50
Fruits & Vegetables			.70			6.00
–Apples	2.20	1.70	1.30	35.50	2.0	17.75
–Grapes	1.75	2.80	.65	20.0	3.50	5.70
–Oranges	2.40	1.15	2.20	30.0	1.75	17.00
–Potatoes	.40	.70	.55	5.50	.80	6.85
–Cabbage	.20	.70	.30	6.0	.75	8.00
–Carrots	.25	.80	.30	5.0	.85	5.90
–Onions	.40	.80	.50	8.50	.85	10.00
Sugar, sweeteners			1.00			14.00
–Powdered sugar	.90	.90	1.00	14.0	1.00	14.00

/1 As of mid–1992

Source: Bank Staff Estimates, 1992

Table 3.5 – Georgia: Georgia's Share in Interrepublic Trade (by commodity)

(As Percent of FSU Total)

	1987	1990
Total Exports	2.97	3.04
Industry	2.94	2.94
–Electricity	0.27	0.65
–Oil and Gas	0.07	0.03
–Coal	0.73	0.42
–Other Fuels	0	0
–Ferrous Metallurgy	2.31	2.09
–Chemical Fuel	1.1	0.51
–Machine Bldg	1.71	1.71
–Timber, wood, pulp and paper	1.23	1.27
–Building materials	1.22	1.15
–Light Industry	4.29	1.78
–Food Industry	10.15	4.09
–Other branches of industry	2.52	10.84
Agriculture	3.89	2.74
Other branches	1.06	5.8
Total Imports	2.65	2.17
Industry	2.64	2.62
–Electricity	2.87	2.54
–Oil and Gas	2.74	2.8
–Coal	1.06	2.15
–Other Fuels	1.2	1.39
–Ferrous Metallurgy	2.75	1.37
–Chemical Fuel	1.75	3.02
–Machine Bldg	2.58	1.66
–Timber, wood, pulp and paper	2.38	2.61
–Building materials	3.88	2.22
–Light Industry	5.02	4.41
–Food Industry	2.68	3.8
–Other branches of industry	2.77	2.8
Agriculture	3.6	2.39
Other branches	2.8	4.16

Table 4.1 – Georgia: Summary State Government Operations, 1991–92
(Millions of Rubles)

	1991 Budget	1991 Actual	1992 Budget	1992 Prel. act
Total Revenue	5267	6198	25100	18872
Tax revenue	3972	4631	22202	15218
Non–Tax Revenue	1295	1567	2898	3655
Total Expenditure	6268	5922	26363	42672
National Economy	2979	2878	11885	20815
Social & Cultural Sphere	2717	2526	10082	12325
Admin & Law Enforcement	245	242	2631	6559
Other Expenditure	327	276	1765	2972
Extrabudgetary expenditure	...	636	12095	22275
Social Security Fund	...	1210	1920	2500
Net Lending	...	575	10175	19775
Errors & Omissions	...	−364	−618	−1046
Primary budget deficit	−1001	−724	−1263	−47120
Interest on Foreign Debt	...	...	...	21714
Central Budget Deficit	−1001	−724	−1263	−68834
Financing	1001	724	1263	68834
Domestic bank credit	...	−276	...	47120
Foreign debt repayment	...	...	...	19200
Debt rescheduling/arrears	...	...	...	−32703
Financing gap/arrears	...	1000	...	54416
Memorandum Items:		(% of GDP)		
Revenue	...	29.8	...	14
Expenditure	...	31.6	...	48.3
Primary Budget Deficit	...	−3.5	...	−35.1
Central Budget Deficit	...	−3.5	...	−51.2

Source: Ministry of Finance, Feb 1993., IMF

Table 4.2 – Georgia: Capital Investment in the State Budget in 1992
(Million Rubles)

		Allocated during 1992			
	Annual Budget	Regular Payments	Natural Disasters	Total Allocated	Percent Allocated
Total State Investment	10573	5344	4741	10085	95
Transport Ministry	1061	1035	14	1050	99
Energy Ministry	1053	1021	13	1034	98
Agriculture Ministry	960	374	525	899	94
Construction Ministry	3128	155	2945	3100	99
Other ministries	4371	2759	1243	4002	92

Source: Ministry of Finance, Main Budget Department

Table 4.3 – Georgia: Public Investment Program, 1991–1992
(Thousands of 1992 Rubles)

Sector	1992 Total Planned	1991 Total Realized	Change (%)
Building materials	150	146	3
Construct. industry	48	130	−64
Light industry	0	31	−100
Printing industry	2	8	−73
Domestic industry	0	15	−100
Auto and transport	12	8	50
Highway construction	550	596	−8
Spec. transport	25	9	166
Aircraft	10	5	104
Oil/oil production	0	41	−100
Communication	112	107	4
Trade	7	23	−71
Housing construction	1398	1480	−6
Communal services	918	716	28
Education	457	364	26
Culture	41	45	−9
Health	363	277	31
Science	30	13	136
Diff. branches	553	256	116
Agroindustry	871	3274	−73
Tbilisi subway	300	286	5
Electroenergy	403	40	908
Coal mining industry	70	...	...
Mission building	10	...	...
Kutaisi Auto plant	...	15	...
Rustavi plant	...	15	...
TOTAL	6329	7902	...

Source: Ministry of Economy, 6 July 1992

Table 5.1 – Georgia: Monetary Survey, 1991–92

(Millions of Rubles)

	Dec 1991	Mar 1992	Jun 1992	Aug 1992	Sep 1992	Oct 1992	Nov 1992	Dec 1992(est)
Net Foreign Assets	76	−1067	−19345	−34394	−64628	−80031	−89493	137150
Foreign Assets	77	1028	10557	25007	26351	35372	44828	51000
Outside Ruble Area	6	123	235	3517	5723	8986	10750	11000
Ruble Area or USSR	71	905	10322	21490	20628	26386	34077	40000
Foreign Liabilities	−1	−2095	−29902	−59401	90979	−115404	−13320	−188150
Outside Ruble Area	−1	−39	−52	−496	−733	−760	−974	−1000
Ruble Area or USSR	...	−2056	−29850	−58905	90246	−114644	−133374	−187150
Ruble Issuance	−6200	−7200	−9851	−15351	−20351	−20351	−32851	−32851
Net Domestic Assets	25476	27080	51230	80915	137878	161314	186948	248000
Domestic Credit	31948	33411	52970	73465	113232	125348	145858	202000
Net claims on State government	12385	13184	16164	19346	35496	38657	40689	62000
Claims on rest of the economy	19563	20227	36806	54118	77736	86681	105170	140000
Nonfinancial Public Enterprises	17095	17040	30979	44659	64391	70284	85260	113470
Private Sector	2468	3187	5827	9460	13345	16397	19909	26530
Other assets	−6472	−6331	−1740	7450	24646	35975	41090	46000
Money Supply	19352	18813	22034	31171	52900	60932	64605	78000
Sberbank Deposits	12575	12575	133888	133888	26766	26766	26766	38000
Time and other deposits	6777	6238	8646	17783	26134	34166	37839	40000

Source: Data provided by NBG; Eximbank; and IMF estimates.

Table 5.2 – Georgia: Cash in Circulation, 1990–92
(Millions of Rubles)

	January – May		
	1990	1991	1992
Inflows to banking system			
Trade	2094.9	2561.3	4123.5
Long–dist. transport	54.6	73.9	232.4
Local transport	79.5	72.6	156.0
Communal services	13.1	18.5	95.3
Entertainment	11.6	8.7	9.2
Small pub. enterpr.	39.0	59.6	106.0
Collectives	9.5	16.3	62.9
Communications	86.4	34.6	...
Savings Bank	547.4	962.1	...
Other inflows	215.8	2071.7	874.7
cooperatives	50.8	146.8	162.5
TOTAL	3151.9	5879.3	5660.0
Outflows from banking system			
Wages	2015.3	2700.9	4588.3
Agro–industry prod.	105.8	334.2	330.3
Collectives' savings	219.5	268.9	324.6
Pensions	148.3	261.9	527.0
Other	562.2	2227.2	861.9
cooperative accts.	518.6	999.0	636.5
Strengthen communic.	0.0	0.0	810.7
Strengthen Sav. Bank	0.0	0.0	472.9
TOTAL	3051.0	5793.2	7915.6
NET INFLOWS OF CURRENCY	100.9	86.2	–2255.6

Source: National Bank of Georgia, July 1992

Table 6.1 – Georgia: Value of Agricultural Production in Constant Prices
(Millions of Rubles, Constant Price)

	1985	1986	1987	1988	1989	1990	1991	1992
Total gross agricultural production	3224.2	3370.7	3140.8	3250.8	2748.2	2937.6	27	050.6
Material inputs	887.5	916.1	913.5	865.2	848.5	932.2	88 0	906.0
Net material product	2336.7	2454.6	2227.3	2385.6	1899.7	2005.4	19	144.

Source: Committee on Social and Economic Information, Feb 1993

Table 6.2 – Georgia: Production and Average Yield of Major Agricultural Crops

	1989	1990	1991	1992
	(Production – thousand tons)			
Grain	332.2	519.4	417.3	450.0
Sunflower seeds	2.6	8.6	10.3	7.8
Sugar beets	39.3	33.6	17.7	15.0
Potatoes	154.2	150.6	102.2	192.5
Vegetables	238.6	183.6	130.1	375.0
Fruits	144.3	119.7	78.6	71.6
Grapes	303.3	379.0	304.5	228.5
Citrus	33.6	46.7	45.6	82.5
Tea	462.4	465.6	400.4	167.3
	(Average yield – kg/ha)			
Grain	19.8	....	18.8	20.3
Sunflower seeds	1.9	6.5	8.7	6.6
Sugar beets	284.8	252.0	153.0	129.7
Potatoes	114.5	100.9	95.8	180.4
Vegetables	102.9	85.7	86.4	249.0
Fruits	34.9	28.8	....	....
Grapes	44.3	57.7	....	....
Citrus	38.5	57.2	50.0	90.5
Tea	86.8	89.2	74.0	30.9

Source: Committee on Social and Economic Indictors, July 1992

Table 6.3 – Georgia: Production and Average Yield of Major Agricultural Crops (Private)

	1989	1990	1991
	(Production – thousands of tons)		
Grain	151.0	173.7	113.7
Sunflower seeds	0.0	0.1	0.1
Sugar beets	...	...	...
Potatoes	148.1	143.2	123.5
Vegetables	276.8	259.6	196.5
Fruits	460.5	471.5	340.0
Grapes	210.3	312.0	213.7
Citrus	60.6	236.4	...
Tea	35.1	36.1	...
	(Average yield–kg/Ha)		
Grain	28.3	30.9	20.6
Sunflower seeds	...	7.9	10.3
Sugar beets	...	...	...
Potatoes	148.6	111.0	98.0
Vegetables	155.5	142.8	128.0
Fruits	77.3	77.7	...
Grapes	58.5	83.6	...
Citrus	70.6	275.4	...
Tea	99.7	102.5	...

Source: Committee on Social and Economic Indicators, Feb 1993

Table 6.4 – Georgia: Main Aggregates of Animal Husbandry Production (Private)
(Thousand Tons)

	1989	1990	1991
Beef	104.0	125.7	125.3
Milk	411.4	402.5	406.2
Eggs	260.7	263.4	262.9

Source: Committee on Social and Economic Indicators, July 1992

Table 6.5 – Georgia: Agricultural Production on State and Private Farms, 1991

	State Production	Private Production	Total Production
	(thousands of 1983 rubles)		
Grain	448	161	609
Sugar beets	9	0	9
Sunflower seeds	27	0	27
Potatoes	196	236	433
Vegetables	406	613	1019
Fruits	457	1907	2364
Grapes	1422	998	2419
Citrus	396	0	396
Tea	3817	0	3817
Beef	1715	279	1994
Eggs	339	252	591
Milk	714	1617	2330
	(As Percentage of Total (%))		
Grain	74	26	100
Sugar beets	100	0	100
Sunflower seeds	100	0	100
Potatoes	45	55	100
Vegetables	40	60	100
Fruits	19	81	100
Grapes	59	41	100
Citrus	100	0	100
Tea	100	0	100
Beef	86	14	100
Eggs	57	43	100
Milk	31	69	100

Source: Committee on Social and Economic Information, Feb 1993

Table 6.6 – Georgia: Sales of Agricultural Products in the Farm Markets, 1992

	Total Sales 1992 (percent of value for same period in 1991)		Prices (rubles)	
	Jan–May	May	Jan–May	May
Total agric. products	94.9	99.4	495.3	524.3
Bread	62.5	57.7	469.4	429.6
Potato	102.1	131.1	521.0	108.8
Vegetables	86.3	83.5	527.7	490.7
Cabbage	99.2	94.8	699.9	832.9
Pickled cabbage	98.8	113.1	336.8	427.0
Onion	156.5	162.9	413.2	420.9
Cucumber	94.7	71.1	402.6	503.7
Pickled cucumber	64.3	67.2	393.2	480.6
Tomato	93.3	108.8	475.4	542.6
Pickled tomato	51.2	49.8	465.7	542.3
Parsley	82.5	61.6	50.9	292.0
Other vegetables	79.9	83.5	527.7	369.1
Fruits and berries	111.2	116.5	499.3	603.3
Apple	132.2	139.5	554.6	654.2
Walnut	70.1	117.4	764.8	779.5
Vegetable oil	217.1	426.4	615.3	550.1
Meat products	94.6	106.5	457.4	543.8
Meat and poultry	86.8	86.2	400.4	500.2
Beef	62.3	67.8	458.1	517.0
Cheese	116.4	159.8	592.1	612.1
Eggs	171.8	242.8	512.3	507.8
Livestock	52.9	127.3	401.0	396.6

Source: Committee on Social and Economic Information.

Report on Social Economic Conditions, June 1992

Table 6.7 – Georgia: Employment in Agriculture
(Thousands)

	1986	1987	1988	1989	1990	1991	1992
Total	738	724	693	653	693	675	663
Collective farms	260	245	230	199	185	154	155
State farms	317	302	290	247	250	233	230
Temporary workers	3	3	3	2	2	2	1
Labor on private plots	158	174	170	204	223	249	240
New Private Cooperatives	..	..	0	1	2	1	2
Private farms	..	..	..	..	31	36	35

Source: Committee for Social & Economic Information, Feb 1993

Table 6.8 – Georgia: Main Indicators of Agricultural Farms

	Total	Collective farms (kolhozes)	State Farms (sovhozes)	Other (state farms)	Private Plots	Private Farms
Number of farms (thousands)	1235	514	569	152	..	..
Gross Output (billion 1983 rubles)	1878	495	358	14	1011	..
Fixed Capital (billion 1983 rubles)	0	..	..	..	..	..
Profits (billion 1983 rubles)	65	79	-14	12	-12	..
Number of loss-making farms	510	218	236	56	..	..
Production (million tons)						
Grain	599	239	194	10	156	..
Sugar beets	19	12	7	0	..	..
Sunflowers	8	7	1	..	0	..
Flax	0	0	..	..	..	..
Potatoes	254	29	78	1	147	..
Vegetables	356	24	95	3	234	..
Meat	212	25	42	4	137	4
Milk	563	95	84	5	365	14
Eggs (billions)	638	42	299	4	287	6
Cattle (millions heads)	1208	196	182	12	779	39
Cows	543	62	55	4	406	16
Pigs	733	104	141	18	459	10
Sheep, goats	1470	471	305	6	684	5
Poultry	20167	1370	6955	304	320	11219

Source: Committee for Social & Economic Information, Feb 1993

Table 7.1 – Georgia: Industrial Production, 1990–92

(thousands of tons, unless otherwise indicated)

	1990	1991	1992
Fuel and energy			
Electric Power (bill of kwh)	14.2	13.4	11.5
Coal	956	698	125
Oil	186	180.9	125
Gas (thousands of m3)	59.9	44.9	12
Gasoline	399	342.4	72
Diesel Fuel	658	494.7	111
Lubricating Oil	3.9	...	...
Mazout	898	763.6	189
Motor Oil	70.5	64.4	5
Metallurgy			
Cast iron	624.8	500.8	242
Steel	1316	961.7	535
Finished Roll Steel	1105	817.9	433
Rolled Ferrous metal	1109	818.1	...
Steel pipes			
in millions of meters	26.7	24.6	12.4
in thousands of tons	499	452.8	207
Manganese ore	1252.6	491	290
Electro–ferro manganese	42.4	55.2	...
Metallurgical manganese (in tons)	1736	1003	...
Machine Building			
A/C motors (thousands of kw)	102	63.3	17.5
Machine tools (units)	1565	1417	987
Electric Welding Equipment			
(thousands of units)	16.1	37.3	...
Magnetic Stations	137	...	...
Flooding Electric Engines	11.3	8.7	...
Lifting motors			
(thousands of units)	22.2	15.6	...
Chemical/Timber Products			
Mineral Fertilizers	130	134.5	76
Chemical fibers & threads	32	20	4.5
Synthetic Ammoniac	219	187.4	117
Synthetic Resin and plastic	40.1	26.4	7.6
Synthetic detergents and soap	17.9	13	...
Sawdust	300	313.1	20
Cellulose	...	...	...
Paper	26.6	20.5	2.1

(continued)

Table 7.1 (cont'd) – Georgia: Industrial Production, 1990–92

(in thousands of tons, unless otherwise indicated)

	1990	1991	1992
Construction			
Asbestos tiles/slates (millions)	26.4	12.6	...
Prefabricated ferro–concrete	1761	1451	138
Building bricks (millions of units)	328	348.3	...
Ceramic Tiles	830	170.6	...
General Merchandise and household appliances			
China and porcelain ware	11.7	5.9	...
Color TV (thousands of units)	50	39.2	7.4
Notebooks (millions of units)	71	39.7	11.2
Light industry			
Silk thread (in tons)	26.8	171.2	...
Cotton Yarn	10.5	6.6	...
Wool Yarn	8	4.1	...
Nonwoven fabrics (mill. of meters)	13	9.8	...
Hosiery (mill. of pairs)	30.2	14.1	9.4
Knitwear (mill. of units)	49.6	24.3	7.2
Footwear (mill. of pairs)	13.3	12.2	2.6
Fabrics, Total (mill. of m2)	110.3	66.5	30.3
Cotton	34.1	16.7	12.9
Wool	9.8	6.1	3.4
Silk	45	27.1	9.7
Other	21.4	16.6	...
Carpets (mill. of m2)	0.8	0.5	0.5
Basic Food stuff			
Granulated Sugar	33.8	11.3	1.2
Meat	69.7	31.2	5.4
Fish	104	56.1	...
Butter	0.8	0.6	0.2
Dairy products	250	151.8	22.5
Fat cheese	16	8.3	2.1
Vegetable Oil	13.8	7.4	0.1
Canned Food	677	385.3	...
Tea, primary processed	127.8	108	...
Natural Tea	120	89.2	30.6
Macaroni Products	21	23.1	18.6
Mineral water (mill of 1/2 liters)	223	158.6	61.3
Cigarettes (thousand mill)	11.2	9.8	5.1
Vodka & Liqueurs	822	774	...
Grape wine	16283	12616	7130
Champagne	18143	13801	9199
Cognac	2165	1460	824

Source: Committee for Social & Economic Information, 1993

Table 7.2 – Georgia: Production of Construction Materials

	units	1987	1988	1989	1990	1991	1992
Cement	ths. tons	1480.7	1351.4	1529.9	1289.8	821.0	1200.0
Azbest–Cement Plates	mln. pcs.	29.6	26.0	35.4	26.0	12.7	32.0
Soft materials for roofs	mln.sq.m.	85.1	86.0	59.8	45.5	15.0	60.0
Glazed Ceramic Plates	ths.sq.m.	935.4	845.0	813.0	678.8	370.0	600.0
Sanitary and Ceramic Means	ths.tons	227.3	206.0	189.5	152.5	90.0	150.0
Linoleum	ths.sq.m.			1133.0	2910.0	1520.0	3000.0
Materials for Walls	mln. bricks	787.8	782.9	805.5	629.0	535.4	669.4
Brick for Construction	mln. bricks	295.6	286.2	271.3	245.1	183.9	329.0
Construction Materials (Artificial)	ths.cub.m.	15791.1	16491.4	17588.9	17583.9	13613.4	14825.0
Sand for Construction Works	ths.cub.m.	5002.4	4862.6	5936.0	3878.2	3202.0	4238.4
Material one fills the holes	ths.cub.m.	671.4	661.1	788.0	702.9	590.0	1070.0

Source: Ministry of Economy, July 1992

Table 8.1 – Georgia: Retail Sales Price Deflators, 1990–92
(Index December 1990 = 100)

	Price Index (period average) Monthly	Percentage Change Month over month	Year over year
1991			
January	103.4	3.4	...
February	106.7	3.2	...
March	113.4	6.3	...
April	161.5	42.4	...
May	161.2	-0.2	...
June	162.5	0.8	...
July	164.8	1.4	...
August	165.1	0.2	...
September	178.6	0.2	...
October	188.5	5.5	...
November	197.3	4.7	...
December	223.0	13.0	123.0
Average 1991	160.5	...	78.5
1992			
January	287.8	29.1	178.3
February	338.1	17.5	216.8
March	1006.9	197.9	787.7
April	1496.5	48.6	826.5
May	1188.7	-20.6	637.4
June	1426.0	20.0	777.6
July	1665.8	16.8	911.0
August	1766.5	6.0	970.0
September	2023.6	14.6	1032.8
October	2257.8	11.6	1098.0
November	2569.1	13.8	1202.0
December	3485.5	35.7	1463.2
Average 1992	1626.0	...	913.1

Source: Committee for Social & Economic Information, Feb 1993

Table 8.2 – Georgia: Retail Sales Price Deflators (by commodity), 1990–92
(Percentage Change Over Comparable Period in Preceeding Year)

	1990 Ann.	1991 Ann.	Jan	Feb	Mar	Apr	May	June	July	August	Sept	Oct	Nov	Dec
				------------------------------ 1992, by month ------------------------------										
General Index	5	79	178	217	788	827	637	777	911	970	1033	1098	1202	1463
Food	7	86	190	120	610	676	516	739	701	825	996	1326	1541	2293
Meat and poultry	9	126	421	678	517	474	447	668	698	488	638	845	605	1182
Vegetable oil	0	34	1052	1391	1504	1304	700	840	843	2253	2332	4630	3414	2173
Milk/dairy products	6	126	189	221	1753	1389	1417	1193	1337	1401	1453	1772	2583	3593
Cheese	0	163	266	...	...	1329	1450	1343	1525	1775	1375	2033	4900	10122
Fruits	22	76	247	379	496	942	983	336	527	494	865	960	1552	860
Eggs	0	63	1059	1054	1054	919	636	781	785	1054	1439	3362	5475	7871
Sugar	0	102	698	857	1815	1614	900	1122	2777	4446	4446	6718	6415	9900
Bread	0	17	2	1056	1060	1300	1041	884	1039	1039	1094	1057	7512	7345
Alcoholic beverages	1	82	135	97	400	243	332	511	347	321	494	534	766	1301
Detergents	3	47	682	746	1467	1573	1602	1729	2160	1170	1114	1110	1532	2260
Tobacco	2	216	290	485	1510	727	602	649	566	527	648	610	823	802
Paper Products	1	60	498	878	885	2170	1042	871	1484	2268	545	694	1743	2011
Metallic home applicance	3	36	366	376	...	1601	1776	1328	1485	1720	1125	1434	850	1595
Electric goods	1	100	181	182	1581	1139	1273	1846	2489	2797	1879	2723	1477	2688
Building materials	2	115	302	347	1420	1342	862	766	954	1458	1187	762	926	1825
Radio/TV equipment	1	63	134	392	1328	1570	874	1263	1292	1196	1150	1359	2331	2216
Medicines/chemicals	1	34	119	168	459	410	1010	772	1070	1077	1110	1109	2058	2364

Source: Committee on Social and Economic Information, Feb 1993

Table 8.3 – Georgia: Market Prices Indices
(Previous Year = 100)

| | 1989 | 1990 | 1991 | | | 1992 | | |
				January	February	March	April	May
Potato	124.8	103.4	303.8	535.3	625.9	545.9	466.5	485.4
Cabbage	115.0	131.2	185.4	509.2	643.4	652.9	654.5	832.9
Onion	123.1	121.5	237.8	406.8	407.6	386.3	395.3	420.9
Garlic	109.4	104.1	299.9	1384.2	1285.3	1651.0	1998.0	23–times
Apple	114.9	121.0	172.9	433.1	504.2	517.8	559.5	654.2
Beef	102.1	134.8	248.0	318.0	409.9	470.9	485.5	517.0
Pig	98.9	126.6	229.8	285.5	337.0	346.7	409.7	517.5
Ham	99.6	138.6	268.0	304.8	301.2	349.5	423.3	482.1
Milk	108.9	139.5	305.9	389.7	352.6	385.3	420.4	419.7
Cheese	109.7	123.6	245.9	409.5	504.4	528.3	714.2	612.1
Eggs	114.4	145.0	255.0	378.5	620.9	509.6	528.2	507.8
Honey	109.2	135.9	317.3	442.6	670.3	851.4	802.4	875.5
Vegetable Oil	82.6	140.2	225.0	457.4	584.8	632.5	554.5	580.1

Source: Committee on Social and Economic Indicators, July 1992

Table 8.4 – Georgia: Administered Prices, 1992

(Rubles)

Product	Unit	Average Price					Change (in percent)		
		Q1	Q2	Q3	Q4	Q1/Q2	Q2/Q3	Q3/Q4
Bread	kg	0.4	4.8	4.8	32.0	1271	0	567
Milk	liter	0.8	5.3	5.3	5.3	571	0	0
Meat	kg	13.1	32.9	free	free	151	...	...
Potatoes	kg	2.0	2.0	free	free	0	...	...
Salt	kg	0.1	3.0	free	free	3650	...	...
Sugar	kg	2.2	18.0	free	free	718	...	...
Vegetable oil	liter	2.1	7.0	free	free	240	...	...
Matches	unit	0.1	1.0	free	free	1900	...	...
Medicines		...	...	...	...	...	...	...
Gasoline (93 Octanes)	liter	0.4	4.8	free	free	1100	...	...
Diesel fuel	liter	0.1	14.0	free	free	19900	...	...
Oil	liter	0.1	6.0	free	free	4515	...	...
Coal	ton	45.0	220.0	set by Russia		389	...	...
Industrial fuel	liter	0.1	7.0	set by Russia		9900	...	...
Natural gas	th. m3	61.0	3000.0	19000.0	...	4818	533	...
Liquid gas	kg	0.3	2.7	10.8	10.8	810	296	0
Electric power	kwh							
Private		0.0	0.1	0.1	1.0	200	0	733
Commercial		0.1	0.5	2.4	2.4	838	363	0
Passenger transport								
Taxi fare	unit	0.2	2.0	6.0	free	900	200	...
Subway	unit	0.1	0.6	1.0	5.0	1100	67	400

Source: Committee for Social and Economic Information, Feb 1993

Table 8.5 – Georgia: Average Wages in 1991–92

(Rubles)

Year	Q1	Q2	Semester I	Q3	Q4	Semester II	1992/1991 (%)
1991	204	271	237	279	350	276	...
1992	...	...	1245	...	5355	3300	1096

Note: The average increase in retail prices in 1992 was 913%.

Source: Report on Social and Economic Situation in Georgia, 1992; IMF

Table 8.6 – Georgia: Minimum Wages 1991–92

(Rubles)

	Jan 91 to Mar 91	Mar 91 to Jan 92	Jan 92 to Feb 92	Feb 92 to May 92	May 92 to Aug 92	Aug 92 to Oct 92	Oct 92 to Nov 92	Nov 92 to Jan 93
In current prices	70	130	260	300	500	650	850	1700
In Dec 1991 prices	71	108	89	88	65	63	77	116

Source: Report on Social and Economic Situation in Georgia 1992.

Distributors of World Bank Publications

ARGENTINA
Carlos Hirsch, SRL
Galeria Guemes
Florida 165, 4th Floor-Ofc. 453/465
1333 Buenos Aires

**AUSTRALIA, PAPUA NEW GUINEA,
FIJI, SOLOMON ISLANDS,
VANUATU, AND WESTERN SAMOA**
D.A. Information Services
648 Whitehorse Road
Mitcham 3132
Victoria

AUSTRIA
Gerold and Co.
Graben 31
A-1011 Wien

BANGLADESH
Micro Industries Development
Assistance Society (MIDAS)
House 5, Road 16
Dhanmondi R/Area
Dhaka 1209

Branch offices:
Pine View, 1st Floor
100 Agrabad Commercial Area
Chittagong 4100

76, K.D.A. Avenue
Kulna 9100

BELGIUM
Jean De Lannoy
Av. du Roi 202
1060 Brussels

CANADA
Le Diffuseur
C.P. 85, 1501B rue Ampère
Boucherville, Québec
J4B 5E6

CHILE
Invertec IGT S.A.
Americo Vespucio Norte 1165
Santiago

CHINA
China Financial & Economic
Publishing House
8, Da Fo Si Dong Jie
Beijing

COLOMBIA
Infoenlace Ltda.
Apartado Aereo 34270
Bogota D.E.

COTE D'IVOIRE
Centre d'Edition et de Diffusion
Africaines (CEDA)
04 B.P. 541
Abidjan 04 Plateau

CYPRUS
Center of Applied Research
Cyprus College
6, Diogenes Street, Engomi
P.O. Box 2006
Nicosia

DENMARK
SamfundsLitteratur
Rosenoerns Allé 11
DK-1970 Frederiksberg C

DOMINICAN REPUBLIC
Editora Taller, C. por A.
Restauración e Isabel la Católica 309
Apartado de Correos 2190 Z-1
Santo Domingo

EGYPT, ARAB REPUBLIC OF
Al Ahram
Al Galaa Street
Cairo

The Middle East Observer
41, Sherif Street
Cairo

FINLAND
Akateeminen Kirjakauppa
P.O. Box 128
SF-00101 Helsinki 10

FRANCE
World Bank Publications
66, avenue d'Iéna
75116 Paris

GERMANY
UNO-Verlag
Poppelsdorfer Allee 55
D-5300 Bonn 1

HONG KONG, MACAO
Asia 2000 Ltd.
46-48 Wyndham Street
Winning Centre
2nd Floor
Central Hong Kong

INDIA
Allied Publishers Private Ltd.
751 Mount Road
Madras - 600 002

Branch offices:
15 J.N. Heredia Marg
Ballard Estate
Bombay - 400 038

13/14 Asaf Ali Road
New Delhi - 110 002

17 Chittaranjan Avenue
Calcutta - 700 072

Jayadeva Hostel Building
5th Main Road, Gandhinagar
Bangalore - 560 009

3-5-1129 Kachiguda
Cross Road
Hyderabad - 500 027

Prarthana Flats, 2nd Floor
Near Thakore Baug, Navrangpura
Ahmedabad - 380 009

Patiala House
16-A Ashok Marg
Lucknow - 226 001

Central Bazaar Road
60 Bajaj Nagar
Nagpur 440 010

INDONESIA
Pt. Indira Limited
Jalan Borobudur 20
P.O. Box 181
Jakarta 10320

IRELAND
Government Supplies Agency
4-5 Harcourt Road
Dublin 2

ISRAEL
Yozmot Literature Ltd.
P.O. Box 56055
Tel Aviv 61560

ITALY
Licosa Commissionaria Sansoni SPA
Via Duca Di Calabria, 1/1
Casella Postale 552
50125 Firenze

JAPAN
Eastern Book Service
Hongo 3-Chome, Bunkyo-ku 113
Tokyo

KENYA
Africa Book Service (E.A.) Ltd.
Quaran House, Mfangano Street
P.O. Box 45245
Nairobi

KOREA, REPUBLIC OF
Pan Korea Book Corporation
P.O. Box 101, Kwangwhamun
Seoul

MALAYSIA
University of Malaya Cooperative
Bookshop, Limited
P.O. Box 1127, Jalan Pantai Baru
59700 Kuala Lumpur

MEXICO
INFOTEC
Apartado Postal 22-860
14060 Tlalpan, Mexico D.F.

NETHERLANDS
De Lindeboom/InOr-Publikaties
P.O. Box 202
7480 AE Haaksbergen

NEW ZEALAND
EBSCO NZ Ltd.
Private Mail Bag 99914
New Market
Auckland

NIGERIA
University Press Limited
Three Crowns Building Jericho
Private Mail Bag 5095
Ibadan

NORWAY
Narvesen Information Center
Book Department
P.O. Box 6125 Etterstad
N-0602 Oslo 6

PAKISTAN
Mirza Book Agency
65, Shahrah-e-Quaid-e-Azam
P.O. Box No. 729
Lahore 54000

PERU
Editorial Desarrollo SA
Apartado 3824
Lima 1

PHILIPPINES
International Book Center
Suite 1703, Cityland 10
Condominium Tower 1
Ayala Avenue, H.V. dela
Costa Extension
Makati, Metro Manila

POLAND
International Publishing Service
Ul. Piekna 31/37
00-677 Warzawa

For subscription orders:
IPS Journals
Ul. Okrezna 3
02-916 Warszawa

PORTUGAL
Livraria Portugal
Rua Do Carmo 70-74
1200 Lisbon

SAUDI ARABIA, QATAR
Jarir Book Store
P.O. Box 3196
Riyadh 11471

**SINGAPORE, TAIWAN,
MYANMAR, BRUNEI**
Information Publications
Private, Ltd.
Golden Wheel Building
41, Kallang Pudding, #04-03
Singapore 1334

SOUTH AFRICA, BOTSWANA
For single titles:
Oxford University Press
Southern Africa
P.O. Box 1141
Cape Town 8000

For subscription orders:
International Subscription Service
P.O. Box 41095
Craighall
Johannesburg 2024

SPAIN
Mundi-Prensa Libros, S.A.
Castello 37
28001 Madrid

Librería Internacional AEDOS
Consell de Cent, 391
08009 Barcelona

SRI LANKA AND THE MALDIVES
Lake House Bookshop
P.O. Box 244
100, Sir Chittampalam A.
Gardiner Mawatha
Colombo 2

SWEDEN
For single titles:
Fritzes Fackboksforetaget
Regeringsgatan 12, Box 16356
S-103 27 Stockholm

For subscription orders:
Wennergren-Williams AB
P. O. Box 1305
S-171 25 Solna

SWITZERLAND
For single titles:
Librairie Payot
Case postale 3212
CH 1002 Lausanne

For subscription orders:
Librairie Payot
Service des Abonnements
Case postale 3312
CH 1002 Lausanne

THAILAND
Central Department Store
306 Silom Road
Bangkok

**TRINIDAD & TOBAGO, ANTIGUA
BARBUDA, BARBADOS,
DOMINICA, GRENADA, GUYANA,
JAMAICA, MONTSERRAT, ST.
KITTS & NEVIS, ST. LUCIA,
ST. VINCENT & GRENADINES**
Systematics Studies Unit
#9 Watts Street
Curepe
Trinidad, West Indies

TURKEY
Infotel
Narlabahçe Sok. No. 15
Cagaloglu
Istanbul

UNITED KINGDOM
Microinfo Ltd.
P.O. Box 3
Alton, Hampshire GU34 2PG
England

VENEZUELA
Libreria del Este
Aptdo. 60.337
Caracas 1060-A

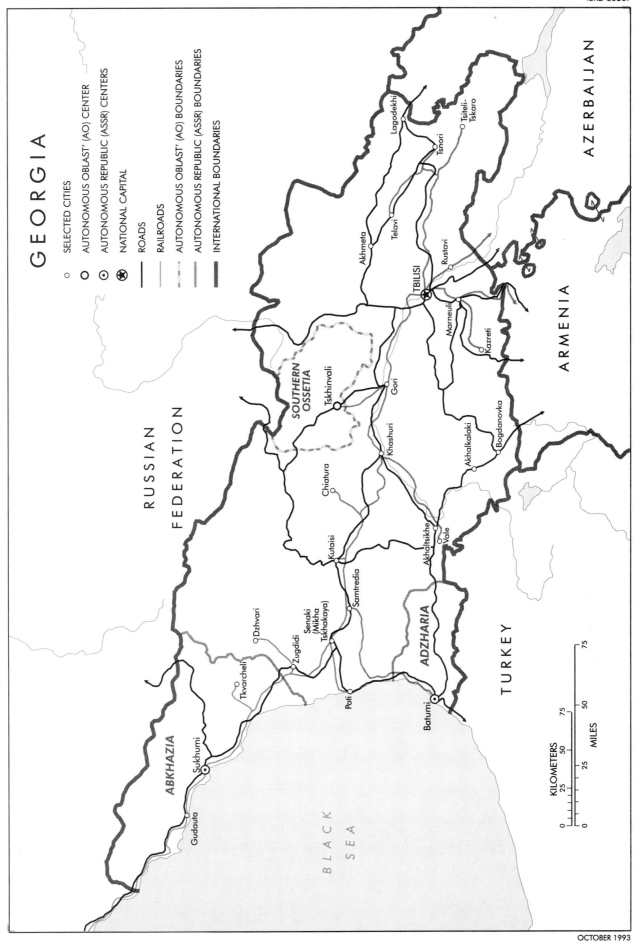

IBRD 25287

GEORGIA

○ SELECTED CITIES
◎ AUTONOMOUS OBLAST' (AO) CENTER
◉ AUTONOMOUS REPUBLIC (ASSR) CENTERS
✪ NATIONAL CAPITAL
── ROADS
── RAILROADS
── AUTONOMOUS OBLAST' (AO) BOUNDARIES
── AUTONOMOUS REPUBLIC (ASSR) BOUNDARIES
── INTERNATIONAL BOUNDARIES

AZERBAIJAN

RUSSIAN

FEDERATION

Lagodekhi
Tsiteli-
Tskaro
Tsnori
Akhmeta
Telavi
Rustavi
TBILISI
Marneuli
SOUTHERN
OSSETIA
Tskhinvali
Kazreti
Gori
Khashuri
Chiatura
Akhalkalaki
Bogdanovka
ARMENIA
Kutaisi
Akhaltsikhe
Vale
Samtredia
Dzhvari
Zugdidi
Senaki
(Mikha
Tskhakaya)
Tkvarcheli
ADZHARIA
Poti
Batumi
TURKEY
ABKHAZIA
Sukhumi
Gudauta

BLACK

SEA

KILOMETERS
0   25   50   75
0   25   50   75
MILES

OCTOBER 1993